D1516239

Mark Templer

The Prayer of the Righteous

DPI

DISCIPLESHIP
PUBLICATIONS
INTERNATIONAL

The Prayer of the Righteous
©2000 by Discipleship Publications International
One Merrill Street, Woburn, MA 01801

Cover design and illustration: Chris Costello
Interior design: Ladislao Mandiola

Printed in the United States of America

ISBN: 1-57782-126-2

To Nadine: You will always be my bride.
  Hannah: I'll always be there to hold you in my arms.
  Luke: You will walk mightily with your God.
  Esther: You are a golden jewel in the hand of God.

Contents

Part 2   Prayers of Impact

Acknowledgments

Writing a book is a labor of love. Writing a book about God can seem to be a task doomed to failure from the beginning, because there is only one book that truly represents God: the Bible. Writing a book about prayer is humbling because it forces me to come face to face with how deeply inadequate I am before God, and how weak my own walk with him really is.

Nonetheless and with my own limitations in mind, I wanted to write this book. I want you to experience God the way I have experienced him. When I was baptized, I had my friend read the account of Legion (Mark 5:1-13) at my baptism. I felt like him—self-destructive, consumed by sin, attracted by Jesus and afraid of him at the same time. I don't feel that way anymore, and I want to share with you what God has given me.

Many people have deeply influenced me. Both my mom and dad and my brother, Erec, did the best they could to help me. I am very grateful for them—for all they have done for me, and for all I learned about God through them. I am sorry for all the ways I have let them down, but I am grateful for the grace of Christ in my life and prayerfully, their grace as well.

Many great authors have moved me deeply. Andrew Murray has written great books on prayer. Paul Y. Cho's *Prayer: Key to Revival*, while undergirded by some problematic theology, is still a thought-provoking book. Dr. J. I. Packer's book, *Knowing God*, is a classic for all time, as is Richard Foster's *Prayer: Finding the Heart's True Home*. Jerry Bridges' recent book, *The Joy of Fearing God*, is also destined to be a classic and has deeply influenced my thinking about God. Max Lucado is a great inspiration and Chuck Swindoll has a masterful understanding of spiritual things. Sam Laing's fantastic book *Be Still, My Soul* has greatly helped me in my walk with God. Douglas Jacoby has opened my mind to the word of God, and the word of God to my mind. My heart has especially opened to who God is and to what heaven is like through Henry Kriete's preaching. With this book, the editorial staff at DPI has been brilliant, giving many helpful suggestions to improve the clarity and power of the material.

I am very grateful to my family—my wife, Nadine, and my kids, Hannah, Luke and Esther—for putting up with me all the time—especially while I was trying to write! Nadine is my inspiration and my encouragement, the love and joy of my life. Many, many kingdom friends have touched my heart and my life. Our dear friends, Douglas and Joyce Arthur, have given us so much through the years and have shown us the cross of Christ, the grace of Christ and the joy of Christ. Kip and Elena McKean have been living examples of what it means to walk in the footsteps of Jesus.

The United Kingdom and Irish churches, especially the London church, have given us their hearts in a wonderful way, and we greatly appreciate the friendships we share with very many here in the UK. The Indian and South Asian brothers and sisters are indelibly etched on our hearts. We will never forget you. We will never forsake you.

I hope you enjoy reading this book as much as I have enjoyed writing it. May it change you forever.

Introduction

'The Prayer of a Righteous Man'

Is any one of you in trouble? He should pray. Is anyone happy? Let him sing songs of praise. Is any one of you sick? He should call the elders of the church to pray over him and anoint him with oil in the name of the Lord. And the prayer offered in faith will make the sick person well; the Lord will raise him up. If he has sinned, he will be forgiven. Therefore confess your sins to each other and pray for each other so that you may be healed. The prayer of a righteous man is powerful and effective.

Elijah was a man just like us. He prayed earnestly that it would not rain, and it did not rain on the land for three and a half years. Again he prayed, and the heavens gave rain, and the earth produced its crops.

James 5:13-18

In this amazing passage of scripture, James concludes his book by teaching that prayer is the best response to almost every problem and situation. He tells us about the miracles God did in answer to Elijah's prayers and astounds us by saying that Elijah was just an ordinary man, like you or me. What a great promise—our prayers can have impact, just like his!

Timeless Desire

From the beginning of time, men have prayed. It is one of our most basic instincts. The soul of man yearns for a relationship with its Creator. Prayer connects us as humans to the realm of God, because when we pray, we leave this world of sin and darkness and enter the throne room of Almighty God.

God deeply desires a relationship with us. He went to great lengths to ensure that we would have a way to reach him: he allowed his own soul and heart to be ripped in two as he watched his one and only Son die on the cross. Jesus' greatest moment of pain on the cross—when he cried out, "My God, my God, why have you forsaken me?" (Matthew 27:46)—came as he was separated from his Father, unable to pray for the first time in his life.

Unlimited Access

In the world, people are thrilled with an autograph, a glimpse of a celebrity, or a brief appointment with someone important. Yet the eternal, omnipotent Creator is willing to give us his attention at any time, in any place we choose. What a tragedy when we fail to take advantage of the indescribable gift of prayer.

Many of us fail to pray because we do not understand God's power and his ability to work in our day to day lives. Prayer is not simply a ritual that we "do" to "stay saved." Indeed, legalistic obedience to rules can lead to a life that Isaiah condemned:

> So then, the word of the Lord to them will become:
>   Do and do, do and do,
>   rule on rule, rule on rule;
>   a little here, a little there—

> *so that they will go and fall backward,*
> *be injured and snared and captured.* (Isaiah 28:13)

But prayer in the Holy Spirit, focused on the purpose of God, can shake the heavens and transform the earth.

Flawed Vision

God loves us very, very much, and he wants us to love him back. He speaks to us through his word and through his finger touching our daily lives. We talk to him in prayer and through the practice of being a living sacrifice for Christ. However, for many people, it is hard to love a God they do not really know. Their view of God is twisted and darkened by their own difficult experiences. Through the psalmist, God says, "you thought I was altogether like you" (Psalm 50:21). But God is not like us, nor is he like our families. He is infinitely better.

I came from a broken home, like many in the world today. My father left when I was ten. I saw him for only a few days for the next fifteen years of my life. Raised by a single mother, I grew self-reliant, rebellious and arrogant, unable to seek a God who seemed very far away, if he existed at all.

My picture of God was flawed. Deep in my heart, I thought he was like my earthly father—distant at best, nonexistent at most times. But our Father in heaven is very different from all that; he is eager to bless us, to love us and to shower blessings upon us.

My view of God began to change when I visited the Church of Christ in Boston. I was attending the Massachusetts Institute of Technology (MIT), and there I met men who knew God—men like Jim Blough, Steve Adkins, Brett Kreider and especially Henry Kriete. As a young believer, the cross broke my heart, and I began to pray. As I saw how God listened to my prayers, I realized how foolish my view of God had been, and I was overwhelmed with gratitude that he could save a wretch like me.

Turning Points

Enoch was an ordinary man, probably living an ordinary life for sixty-five years. However, after he became a father, he "walked with God" (Genesis 5:21-24). Perhaps it was the image of his precious son Methusaleh, cradled in his arms, that made him appreciate his heavenly Father. But one thing is clear—there was a *turning point* in his walk with God. He permanently changed. And he walked with God three hundred years, until God took him away to glory.

For me, that turning point occurred when I was a disciple at MIT. One day my Bible discussion leader, Brett Kreider, spent about two hours with me, teaching me how to pray by praying together with me. At that time, there were three sincere young men who had been coming to the Bible discussion group for months, but still had not made their decisions for Christ. Everyone had met with them to encourage and inspire them, but still they did not budge. So, I decided to pray (as I am sure others were also doing). With desperation and consistency, I begged God for their souls. I had quiet times in which I was radical and felt I had really connected with God. Soon after one such quiet time, during one weekend, both Mark Shelley and Carl Pietrzak made decisions to follow Jesus and were baptized into Christ. (Mark is now married to Julie, and together they lead the church in Boise, Idaho.) A few weeks later, Kevin Hurst also decided, suddenly, to repent and be baptized. (He is doing great as a disciple to this day.)

I was convinced—not only was God real, but he actually would listen to me. My prayers could make an impact on the world, because God is great—and he listens to me! This was a turning point that changed me forever. I saw that Jesus was distraught that his disciples could not even pray for one hour in the garden of Gethsemane (Mark 14:32-42), so I decided to pray for at least an hour, every day, for the rest of my life. Fifteen years have passed, and I have not missed a day. And I feel incredibly close to a wonderful Father in heaven who loves me, takes care of me and lives in me through his Spirit.

What to Expect

I am writing this book in the hope that many who read it will have a similar turning point in their spiritual lives. (You may not come to the same conclusions as I, for we are not *commanded* to pray for any specific length of time each day. But we all need to make radical decisions that will draw us closer to God in prayer.) We are held back by our sins, our dysfunctional pasts and our distorted views of a small or distant God who is either helpless or uninterested in our lives. This is far from the truth! Part 1 of this book paints a picture of the God we need to fall in love with, the God who desperately desires a divine romance with each of us. Part 2 explains how we can each have a prayer life with impact that shakes the world around us. Let us be done with token quiet times, ritualistic prayers and small vision! Let us decide to change the world together through the power of our awesome God!

PART 1

God Is Great,
and That's a Fact

1

God Is Running Through the Fields

"Suppose one of you has a hundred sheep and loses one of them. Does he not leave the ninety-nine in the open country and go after the lost sheep until he finds it? And when he finds it, he joyfully puts it on his shoulders and goes home. Then he calls his friends and neighbors together and says, 'Rejoice with me; I have found my lost sheep.'"

Luke 15:4-6

"But while he was still a long way off, his father saw him and was filled with compassion for him; he ran to his son."

Luke 15:20b

Prayer starts with the right view of God. In Luke 15, Jesus told a parable to help his disciples understand his Father's heart. A sheep had wandered off. The shepherd then had one thing on his mind—he went after the sheep until he found it (v5). He ran through the fields, over the hills, searching with all his heart. He was probably covered in sweat with mud on his shoes or filling his sandals. But when he found the sheep, he was very excited. He bent over, put the dirty sheep on his shoulders, ran back through the fields and met his neighbors. He then threw an incredible party to celebrate.

God is the shepherd. We are the lost sheep. He has gone to great efforts just to have a relationship with you and me. He thinks we are worth it. When we understand this, it is much easier to pray.

Painful Memories

My dad grew up with a father who worked hard, but did not spend much time with his children. My father imitated his father's example—he did not know any better—so when I came along, he did not make much time for me. In ten years together, the only shared experience I can remember is going to the movie *The Planet of the Apes* together. That was it. When I was ten, he decided to leave. I laid outside his bedroom on the floor, crying, begging for him to stay. But he left, and I barely saw him for the next fifteen years. Though I did not know it at the time, these events deeply influenced my heart and my view of God.

My dad did not "run through the fields" for me. I had to find my way by myself. Growing up with a single mom, I learned to be tough. She worked very hard to take care of us, but times were hard. I did not believe in God—certainly not in a God who cared for me—and it was hard for me to pray.

Some of you are in the same situation. Your background has given you the wrong view of God, and you are not motivated to pray. However, we need to understand that God is *not* far away and uninterested; he is running through the fields, ready to do anything to have a relationship with us.

Seeing God's Hand

Jesus traveled all the way from heaven to come to the earth. He endured the full life of a human being, suffering incredibly, just to give us a chance to be saved. He also has gone to great efforts in each of our lives so that we could have a relationship with his Father. In Acts 17:26-27, we learn that God has arranged the times and places where men should live, that they should seek him and reach out for him and find him. This scripture applies to nations in human history, but I believe these verses are also about individuals. Indeed, "he is not far from each one of us."

In my life, I can clearly see that God was running after me. As a child, I was very interested in mathematics, especially prime numbers. When I was about fifteen, an article on prime numbers appeared in *Time* magazine, mentioning MIT as a leading center of mathematics research. Shortly after this, someone asked me where I was planning to go for university. I had never thought about it before, but since I had read the magazine article, I said "MIT." After that, I always intended to go there.

Taking It Personally

Douglas Arthur led the MIT campus ministry of the Boston Church of Christ in the summer of 1981. He came up with the ministry plan of knocking on every door on campus and inviting every student that summer to come to a local Bible discussion group. Though I did not come, I always remembered the guys who invited me, Don Murray and Jeff Zimmer. They called me frequently, but still I did not attend, and eventually they gave up.

The next summer I was involved in two near-miss automobile accidents that rattled me deeply and made me think about God, life and death. Also, years earlier, I had been very interested in English literature and Shakespeare, and during the summer of 1982, I developed a curiosity about the famous book I had not read at all—the Bible. God was working in many areas of my life, trying to pull me to him.

A few months later, I was burdened about some of my relationships at MIT, and I remembered Don. I saw him on campus and asked if he still had his Bible discussion group—he was amazed and encouraged that I asked. When I went to the Bible discussion, led by Jim Blough and Jeff Zimmer, it was incredible! Thus, I began my spiritual journey.

For fifteen months I attended church activities and events without making a decision for Christ. As I slowly came to believe in God, I began to reflect on the incredible "coincidences" that led me to learn about Jesus. I read in the Bible how much God loved each person, and I could see how he had loved me personally, running through the fields just to give me a chance. Other than my mother, I had never known anyone who loved me as much as he did. I fell in love with this God, I was baptized into Christ, and my life has never been the same! This same God has run through the fields for you, too.

TAKING INVENTORY

1. How did your experiences growing up shape your view of God? What changes in your view did you make in order to become a disciple?

2. How has your view of God changed since your baptism?

3. How did God run after you?

2

God Is Crawling
on His Knees

*"Or suppose a woman has ten silver coins and loses
one. Does she not light a lamp, sweep the house and
search carefully until she finds it?"*

Luke 15:8

Jesus paints another picture of God in Luke 15. A woman
has lost a coin, and she is desperate to find it. She lights a
lamp, gets a broom and sweeps everywhere, searching for
the coin. She crawls on her knees, reaching underneath the
furniture, searching for the coin. She is covered in dust, with
dirt under her fingernails, but still she keeps looking until
she finds that coin. It does not matter to her that she has nine
others; she wants *that* coin. This is how God humbled and
dirtied himself, just to search for one lost soul—you!

Paul, in Philippians 2:7-8, said that Jesus humbled
himself, making himself nothing, just to die on the cross.
The New American Standard Bible says simply that Jesus
"emptied himself." By grace, Jesus, who was rich, became
poor for us (2 Corinthians 8:9). He became sin for us
(2 Corinthians 5:21). He was willing to get dirty, to come

down to our level. Jesus is able to sympathize with our weaknesses and was tempted in every way, just as we are, yet was without sin (Hebrews 4:15-16). Jesus got on his knees to wash the disciples' feet (John 13:1-5). As a carpenter and the son of a carpenter, he must have frequently gotten down on his knees to pick up nails. Truly, our God is crawling on his knees!

The Masks We Wear

Even after we realize that God has crawled on his knees for us, some of us feel distant from him. We are so ashamed of our sins and failures that we think he could never accept us just as we are. We have been rejected before, and we are afraid it will happen again. So we wear a religious mask, and we are empty inside. The Beatles sang about someone like this in the song "Eleanor Rigby":

> Eleanor Rigby picks up the rice in a church,
> Where a wedding has been.
> Lives in a dream.
> Waits at the window, wearing a face that she keeps
> In a jar by the door.
> Who is it for?

Peter was afraid when Jesus first got close to him. In Luke 5:8, he said, "Go away from me, Lord; I am a sinful man!" Peter was wearing a mask of religion. When Jesus started getting too close, he was afraid.

Legion, the demoniac in the region of the Gerasenes, ran to Jesus when he saw him (Mark 5:6). But when Jesus rebuked his evil spirit, he shouted, "What do you want with me, Jesus, Son of the Most High God? Swear to God that you won't torture me!" (Mark 5:7-8). Legion was wearing a mask of anger and violence and self-destructive habits to hide the pain inside his heart. When Jesus got too close, he also was afraid. Some of us wear masks. We like Jesus, but we are afraid of letting him get too close to our lives. We feel too sinful to let him in. Also, we do not have great relationships with people, because no one really knows us. And we are so afraid of rejection that we are not close to God.

A God's Eye View of Sin

The God of the Bible is crawling on his knees, reaching into the slime to pull us out. David prayed, "rescue me from the mire, do not let me sink" (Psalm 69:14). David said, "you stoop down to make me great" (Psalm 18:35). He also said:

> I waited patiently for the Lord;
>   he turned to me and heard my cry.
> He lifted me out of the slimy pit,
>   out of the mud and mire;
> he set my feet on a rock
>   and gave me a firm place to stand. (Psalm 40:1-2)

A few months ago, our bathtub was leaking through the ceiling into our ground floor because the drain was clogged. We tried crystals, but the drain remained clogged. So we followed the drainpipe outside the house. It went into a box that was nailed shut—but water was leaking out of the box. Without thinking, I pried the box partially open, loosening some of the nails. I reached into the box, groping around with my bare hand. I found the drain. It was covered in slime, clogged by hair and grime. I fully removed the box cover to get inside to clean it, and I was completely disgusted by what I saw. Dozens of worms and slugs of every kind covered it on the bottom. Using plastic bags, one by one, I removed them, cleaning up the drain. I replaced it and nailed the box shut. My hands were so dirty. I had to wash them for several minutes to remove the grime and that stench.

As disgusting as this experience was to me, this is a small example of how God feels about sin. Indeed, in Ezekiel 8:10 he showed Ezekiel the idolatry of Israel's religious leaders, and Ezekiel saw "all kinds of crawling things and detestable animals." Some of us have a box like my drain box in our lives. It is locked shut, and the sin is hidden away. But God wants to get in and clean it up. He is willing to get dirty, to get involved with the real you.

That dirty drain was my life before I became a Christian—impressive on the outside (in some ways), but full of slime. I did not trust anyone. I was full of lust, bitterness, deceit, guilt and anger. When I finally opened up and confessed my sins, what an incredible relief it was. I was free at last! As a Christian, I have had to repeatedly clean up the slime by regularly confessing my sins. I am not what I ought to be. But I am not what I used to be, and God loves me, and he is crawling on his knees for me. I can pray to a God like that!

God wants to clean you up. He will not reject you, no matter how dirty you are. Let him in, and he will change your life.

TAKING INVENTORY

1. Psalm 66:17-19 speaks about how the psalmist prayed and God listened because he did not cherish sin in his heart. What about you? Do you have a locked box that no one knows about? When will you open up with other disciples about your sin?

2. Are you afraid of rejection to the point that you find it difficult to pray? Whether yes or no, what are some good scriptures with which to combat this fear?

3. Do you believe God can forgive you, without you earning it? In what ways do you try to "earn" his forgiveness? How will you change?

3

God Is Throwing Open His Arms

"So he got up and went to his father.
But while he was still a long way off, his father saw
him and was filled with compassion for him; he ran to
his son, threw his arms around him and kissed him."
Luke 15:20

The story of the father welcoming his lost son home is one of the most moving in all of Scripture. It is the story of each of our lives before we changed and came back to God. It shows us the very heart of God and motivates us to love him and forgive others. God is throwing open his arms to forgive us, no matter what we have done. The father threw open his arms to his son *before* he apologized, before hearing how he had changed, because he was so glad his son was coming home. His forgiveness was unconditional.

Wild Living

The scene described in Luke 15:12-13 is incredibly sad. The younger son did not appreciate what he had at home with his father and family. He realized his father was getting older, and perhaps one day he thought to himself, *Someday Dad will die, and then I will get part of his estate.* As the years passed, this thought grew in his mind. Finally, one day he boldly approached his father and insensitively asked for his share of the inheritance. He was not thinking of how his father would feel; he only thought of his own desires. Amazingly, his father graciously complied with his request.

With the money he received, the son went to a faraway country. There he wasted all that his father had given him. His life was full of sin (Luke 15:13, 30). At the same time that he ran out of money, that country's economy collapsed—there was a severe famine (v14). He was forced to take a humiliating job working in the fields, feeding the pigs (which were unclean according to Old Testament laws). He was not well paid, and he was so hungry that he was jealous of the pigs' food (vv15-16).

Sitting with the pigs, he had time to think. Perhaps he remembered the happy times with his family, eating together. He remembered how he and his dad would work together in the fields. He remembered the singing and the laughter and the kindness of his home far away. But that was a long time ago. He was incredibly ashamed of what he had done—he was reluctant to go home.

A Revelation

At last he came to his senses. He remembered the way his dad treated the hired men, with generosity and kindness (v17). He thought, in essence, *I am not worthy of being a son, but at least as a servant in my father's house, I will be better off than this* (vv18-19). Max Lucado beautifully describes what this moment may have been like in *Six Hours One Friday*:

> Something told him that this was the moment of—and for—truth.

He looked into the water. The face he saw wasn't pretty—muddy and swollen. He looked away. "Don't think about it. You're no worse off than anybody else. Things will get better tomorrow."

The lies anticipated a receptive ear. They'd always found one before. "Not this time," he muttered. And he stared at his reflection.

"How far I have fallen." His first words of truth. He looked into his own eyes. He thought of his father. "They always said I had your eyes." He could see the look of hurt on his father's face when he told him he was leaving.

"How I must have hurt you."

A crack zigzagged across the boy's heart.

A tear splashed into the pool. Another soon followed. Then another. Then the dam broke. He buried his face in his dirty hands as the tears did what tears do so well; they flushed out his soul.

His face was still wet as he sat near the pool. For the first time in a long time he thought of home. The memories warmed him. Memories of dinner table laughter. Memories of a warm bed. Memories of summer evenings sitting on the terrace with his father as they listened to the hypnotic ring of the crickets.

"Father." He said the word aloud as he looked at himself. "They used to say I looked like you. Now you wouldn't even recognize me. Boy, I blew it, didn't I?"

He stood up and began to walk.[1]

So the lost son took his first steps home. He was ready to apologize.

Anticipation

Meanwhile, his father was home, working—but he was also waiting. Luke 15:20 says the father saw him while he

---

[1]Max Lucado, *Six Hours One Friday* (Portland, Oregon: Multnomah Press, 1989), 102-103.

was still a long way off. He was waiting and longing for his lost son. Perhaps for years he had scanned the horizon, hoping to see the distant silhouette of his son returning home. On one particular day, his dream came true! He ran through the fields. He threw open his arms and embraced his son with a warmth and passion that melted away years of pain. Then he threw the mother of all parties to welcome his son home. No expense was spared (vv22-24). It was an incredible celebration. The point of the story? This is how our Father in heaven feels about us when we come home.

Body Language 101

When someone greets you, their arms tell a story. Are they folded, pushing you away? Are they stiffly shaking your hand, keeping you at arm's length? Are they awkwardly giving you a reluctant hug? Or are they thrown open to welcome and hug you? God's arms are open wide, showing how our Father feels about us when we come home. They are open wide to welcome sinners who do not deserve it.

Jesus literally opened wide his arms for us on the cross. In Romans 10:21, God says, "All day long I've held out my hands to a disobedient and obstinate people." He opens wide his arms, simply hoping that sinners will come back to him. God's heart is a pleading heart, begging us to change. At Pentecost, Peter pleaded with the people to be saved (Acts 2:40). In Hosea 11:8, God cries out:

> *"How can I give you up, Ephraim?*
> *How can I hand you over, Israel?*
> *How can I treat you like Admah?*
> *How can I make you like Zeboiim?*
> *My heart is changed within me;*
> *all my compassion is aroused." (Hosea 11:8)*

Our God cares deeply for us. His heart was filled with pain at the sin of the people in the days of Noah (Genesis 6:6). It breaks his heart today when we are in pain, when we fight with each other, when we are far from him.

Some of us do not really believe we can be forgiven. We look at our sins, and we despair. Maybe you never felt forgiven growing up, or maybe you have had trouble forgiving someone else. You need to look at God's forgiveness: his arms are wide open, eagerly welcoming us into his embrace. Understanding this will help you to pray like never before.

Bitter Roots

In the parable of Luke 15, the older son did not spread out his arms to welcome his brother. His first reaction to his brother's return, and his dad's warm welcome, was to become angry. So the dad pleaded with him (v28), but he was mad at his dad. He was bitter about having to obey without ever receiving the blessings he thought he deserved (v29). He refused to call his brother, "my brother," referring to him instead as "this son of yours" (v30). The father wanted both of his sons back with him—and back with each other. He threw open his arms equally wide for both, but only one was able to hug him back.

Some of us have difficulty praying because we are angry with God. We are like the older son—we feel that God owes us something, and in spite of our faithfulness, he has not blessed us the way we think he should. We have forgotten the God of the Bible whose arms are open wide for us. Let us make sure we do not fold our arms to him.

Some of us are like the older brother in that we harbor resentments and attitudes toward our brothers and sisters in Christ. They may have sinned against God and us, and we feel that God has not brought about justice. Of course in Luke 18:7-8, Jesus promises justice for his people but questions whether we will have the faith to persevere in prayer.

Justice will come, but on God's timetable, not ours! Are you willing to wait? Are you willing to forgive? You will never be able to draw close to God, no matter how much you pray, if there is bitterness in your heart.

Matthew 5:23-24 teaches that we are to *first* be reconciled to our brother, and only then should we offer our gifts at the altar. In 1 Peter 3:7 husbands are admonished to treat their wives in a considerate and respectful way, "so that nothing will hinder your prayers." If you have ever tried to pray after sinning against and fighting with your spouse, you know how true this verse is! One of the things I appreciate most about my wife, Nadine, is that she does not hold resentments in her heart. She speaks her mind, and we can talk, forgive and be reconciled. We are reconciled quickly to each other and to God. If you let the sun go down on your anger (Ephesians 4:26), you cannot have a great daily walk with God.

If we cannot throw our arms open to welcome the people around us, we are not being like God, and we cannot get close to him, no matter how much we pray. He will not hear our prayers. If we do not forgive others, he will not forgive us (Matthew 6:15, 18:33-35). Indeed, Jesus' parable in Matthew 18:21-35 is not told simply to achieve superficial reconciliation in our relationships on earth, but to make sure our hearts are right before God. Surface reconciliation on earth with an unforgiving heart is not good enough for God.

God is throwing his arms wide open. It is time to run, with our arms open, into his embrace. He will never let you go!

TAKING INVENTORY

1. In what ways were you like the prodigal son in the parable before you became a disciple? As a disciple, how are you like the older son? How will you change?

2. What bitterness, sin or lack of forgiveness is currently distracting your prayers? How soon will you resolve these things?

3. Do you keep thinking about those who have hurt you? Are your arms folded so tightly that you cannot open them wide to receive God's embrace? (Remember that whoever has sinned against you, his or her sin is not worth ruining your own relationship with God.)

4

God Is Carrying Me in His Arms

He tends his flock like a shepherd:
He gathers the lambs in his arms
and carries them close to his heart;
he gently leads those that have young.

Isaiah 40:11

Preachers often have scriptures of which they say, "This is my favorite passage in all the Bible." The above is one of mine. It is the illustration Jesus alludes to in the Parable of the Lost Sheep (Luke 15). The shepherd picks up the lost sheep and carries it home. As he carries the lamb, it is "close to his heart" (Isaiah 40:11). This is how God feels about us and how he treats us. After he has run through the fields to find us, crawled on his knees to pick us up and thrown open his arms to forgive us, he carries us home in his arms.

Arms of Comfort

I weep when I think of the picture Jesus paints of the death of Lazarus. The poor, old, dirty beggar, covered in sores, without hope, dies alone. But the angels come and tenderly bring him to God (Luke 16:19-22). In heaven he rests "in his [Abraham's] bosom" (Luke 16:23, NASB). It comforts me tremendously that when we die as Christians, the angels carry us home to God.

Most parents have experienced the joy of comforting their crying child by holding the child in their arms. I still remember falling and dislocating my elbow when I was three or four years old. My mother carried me safely to a friend's car and then to the hospital. Held safe in the arms of a parent, a child feels secure. The little one does not need to cry—everything is going to be okay. Most children walking along a road instinctively reach out to grasp the hand of a parent.

A child who is not regularly cuddled is deeply damaged by this experience. We have a lovely adopted child, Esther. We welcomed her into our home when she was six months old. Though the orphanage that housed her was an excellent facility, it could not take the place of her mother and father. Esther loves cuddling with us. She loves being carried—by us and by everyone else, too. It is unlikely that Esther's mom gave her much affection when she was born. We know from the nuns at the orphanage that her mother gave her away without ever even holding her. There is nothing we can do to change Esther's past. But we are going to hold her now until she knows everything will be okay. Amazingly, God expresses this parental love toward us in Isaiah 66:13: "As a mother comforts her child, so will I comfort you."

Arms of Protection

> "Even to your old age and gray hairs I am he,
>   I am he who will sustain you.
> I have made you and I will carry you;
>   I will sustain you and I will rescue you." (Isaiah 46:4)

Sadly, many of us think about God, and we wonder, "Does he really carry me?" Many of us have lost the confidence that "God will protect me." Our lives are frantic, full of activities and without the peace of God. The following passages remind us that God is carrying us in his arms, and that God says, "Do not be anxious—I will take care of it."

> *The Lord is near. Do not be anxious about anything, but in everything, by prayer and petition, with thanksgiving, present your requests to God. And the peace of God, which transcends all understanding, will guard your hearts and your minds in Christ Jesus. (Philippians 4:5b-7)*

> *Cast all your anxiety on him because he cares for you. (1 Peter 5:7)*

> *"Fear not, for I have redeemed you;*
> *   I have summoned you by name; you are mine.*
> *When you pass through the waters,*
> *   I will be with you;*
> *and when you pass through the rivers,*
> *   they will not sweep over you.*
> *When you walk through the fire,*
> *   you will not be burned;*
> *   the flames will not set you ablaze." (Isaiah 43:1-2)*

God promises to take hold of the hands of his kings (Isaiah 45:1) and his people (Isaiah 42:6). He takes care of the birds, the grass and the flowers (Matthew 6:26-30). He will take care of you and me.

Martha or Mary?

Most likely, you used to hold your mom's or dad's hand, and enjoyed their warm embrace. But then you grew up and had to learn to take care of yourself. You left home. Mom and Dad were far away—or maybe they never were very close, and you learned quickly to take care of yourself. (You also learned the meaning of stress!) Most likely, you can relate to Martha in Luke 10:38-42. Jesus went to the home of Mary and Martha, and Martha was busy serving, getting dinner ready. She was distracted by the details of life so that she missed the chance to sit at the feet of Jesus, like her sister, Mary, did. She missed the peace that passes understanding. Mary indeed chose what was better.

I can relate to Martha. I think too much. I want it all done, now! I do not want to leave anything to chance—oh, do I need God! Time in prayer is time when I can quiet my anxious soul, and remember Psalm 46:10, "Be still, and know that I am God." I am learning not to do it all myself. I am learning to do my best and to let God do the rest. Jesus said:

> *"Come to me, all you who are weary and burdened, and I will give you rest. Take my yoke upon you and learn from me, for I am gentle and humble in heart, and you will find rest for your souls." (Matthew 11:28-29)*

God wants to carry us in his arms. Let us climb up, and enjoy the ride!

Footprints

One night a man had a dream.

He dreamed he was walking along the beach with the Lord.

Across the sky flashed scenes from his life.

For each scene, he noticed two sets of footprints in the sand: one belonging to him, and the other to the Lord.

When the last scene of his life flashed before him, he looked
back at the footprints in the sand.
He noticed that many times along the path of his life there
was only one set of footprints.
He also noticed that it happened at the very lowest and
saddest times in his life.

This really bothered him and he questioned the Lord about it.
"Lord, you said that once I decided to follow you, you'd
walk with me all the way.
But I have noticed that during the most troublesome times
in my life, there is only one set of footprints.
I don't understand why when I needed you most you would
leave me.

The Lord replied, "My son, my precious child, I love you
and would never leave you.
During your times of trial and suffering, when you see only
one set of footprints, it was then that I carried you.

–Anonymous

TAKING INVENTORY

*1. Think back and remember a time when, as a child, you
really needed comfort. Was someone there to comfort you
or not? How did that feel?*

*2. What is your favorite verse of comfort? Write it out. If you
don't have one, find one today and begin to memorize it.*

*3. Do you relate more to Martha or Mary? Ask your close
friends who they think you are more like. What do you need
to change as a result of asking this question?*

5

God Is Wiping Away the Tears

And I heard a loud voice from the throne saying, "Now the dwelling of God is with men, and he will live with them. They will be his people, and God himself will be with them and be their God. He will wipe every tear from their eyes. There will be no more death or mourning or crying or pain, for the old order of things has passed away."

Revelation 21:3-4

Our world is full of pain. The twentieth century was perhaps the bloodiest of all time, with tens of millions of innocents slaughtered in Stalin's gulags, Mao's cultural revolution, Hitler's concentration camps and the bloodbaths in Cambodia, Rwanda and Yugoslavia. Wars, famines, natural disasters—the pain of the human race continues to escalate unabatedly, even as technological advances make the lives of the rich ever more comfortable. Divorce, broken homes, child abuse, drug abuse, murder, rape, incest—millions live in a private hell, trapped in a terrible reality or held prisoner by memories of a horrible past. There are rivers of tears to wipe away.

'You Will Have Trouble'

Some of us only see suffering from a distance. It seems to have fortuitously passed us by—for the moment. It is hard for us to understand why. Yet when suffering hits us, suddenly, in all its force, it can be overwhelming. We can either drop to our knees in prayer, or we can choose to run away from God. Elihu observed in Job 35:9-10:

> *"Men cry out under a load of oppression;*
> *they plead for relief from the arm of the powerful.*
> *But no one says, 'Where is God my Maker…?'"*

Paul, however, chose to run to God, as he explained in 2 Corinthians 1:8b-9:

> *We were under great pressure, far beyond our ability to endure, so that we despaired even of life. Indeed, in our hearts we felt the sentence of death. But this happened that we might not rely on ourselves but on God, who raises the dead.*

Suffering is a language that God understands. Elihu said in Job 36:15, "But those who suffer he delivers in their suffering; he speaks to them in their affliction." Indeed, Jesus was "a man of sorrows, and familiar with suffering" (Isaiah 53:3). About Jesus, Hebrews 2:18 says that "because he himself suffered when he was tempted, he is able to help those who are being tempted." Because God understands our suffering, he wants to wipe away our tears.

God Suffers, Too

The gospel is the story of God's suffering. He made this awesome world. Then we all rejected him. The Parable of the Tenants (Matthew 21:33-46) tells the story of the rejection of God. After the tenants rejected his servants, one after another, God only had his son left to send (vv35-36). So he sent his son (v37). And we murdered him. The result? God was shattered and bleeding. He felt our pain. He understands what it means to not be whole.

Because God has given men freedom to choose, there is suffering on earth. It breaks God's heart, but he uses it for our benefit. When we do suffer, it gives us a unique chance to draw close to God. There is a unique bond between those who suffer and those who comfort them in that suffering. God wants to have that special bond with you and me. He wants to wipe away our tears. It is the same kind of bond that he has with his Son. As Jesus said, "Blessed are those who mourn, for they will be comforted" (Matthew 5:4).

Templers in Auschwitz

Each of us needs to be aware of God as we suffer. We also need to be grateful that he has spared us from far greater suffering than we have already experienced. My own family's background deeply moves me to appreciate the mercy of God in my life. Around 1906, at the high point of immigration from eastern and southern Europe to the United States, two Jewish tailors came as young men from the Carpathian Mountains of Galicia in southern Poland (near Krakow, then part of Austria) to settle in Chicago. One, Isisdor Templer, was the father of Robert Nathan Templer; the other, Peretz Maltz, was the father of Robert's future wife, Lillian. Robert worked as a manager of a movie theatre. Lillian, a fellow Polish Jew, worked as the cashier there, and they fell in love. They married during the Great Depression and had children. This couple was Robert and Lillian Templer, my dad's parents. Meanwhile, back in Poland, their cousins, uncles, aunts, nephews and nieces were being herded into ghettos, and eventually into concentration camps—especially Auschwitz.

Countless Jews from Poland perished at Auschwitz, including many from Galicia.[1] One Italian Jew who survived Auschwitz encountered a Templer there. Primo Levi wrote in *Survival at Auschwitz*:

> But it is not only because of the sun that today is a happy day: at midday a surprise awaits us. Besides the normal morning ration, we discover in the hut a wonderful pot of over eleven gallons, one of those from the Factory Kitchen, almost full. Templer looks at us, triumphant; this "organization" is his work.
>
> Templer is the official organizer of the Kommando: he has an astonishing nose for the soup of civilians, like bees for flowers. Our Kapo, who is not a bad Kapo, leaves him a free hand, and with reason: Templer slinks off, following imperceptible tracks like a bloodhound, and returns with the priceless news that the Methanol Polish workers, one mile from here, have abandoned ten gallons of soup that tasted rancid, or that a wagonload of turnips is to be found unguarded on the siding next to the Factory Kitchen.
>
> Today there are ninety pints and we are fifteen, Kapo and *Vorarbeiter* included. This means six pints each: we will have two at midday as well as the normal ration, and will come back to the hut in turns for the other four during the afternoon, besides being granted an extra five minutes' suspension of work to fill ourselves up.
>
> What more could one want? Even our work seems light, with the prospect of four hot, dense pints waiting for us in the hut. The Kapo comes to us periodically and calls: *"Wer hat noch zu fressen?"* He does not say it from derision or to sneer, but because this way of eating on our feet, furiously, burning our mouths and throats, without time to

---

[1] Primo Levi, *Survival at Auschwitz*, trans. by Stuart Woolf (London: Simon & Schuster, 1993), 68.

breathe, really is *"fressen,"* the way of eating of animals, and certainly not *"essen,"* the human way of eating, seated in front of a table, religiously. *"Fressen"* is exactly the word, and is used currently among us.

Meister Nogalla watches and closes an eye at our absences from work. Meister Nogalla also has a hungry look about him, and if it was not for the social conventions, perhaps he would not despise a couple of pints of our warm broth.

Templer's turn comes. By plebiscitary consensus, he has been allowed ten pints, taken from the bottom of the pot. For Templer is not only a good organizer, but an exceptional soup-eater...

At sunset, the siren of the *Feierabend* sounds, the end of work; and as we are all satiated, at least for a few hours, no quarrels arise, we feel good, the Kapo feels no urge to hit us, and we are able to think of our mothers and wives, which usually does not happen. For a few hours we can be unhappy in the manner of free men."[2]

Perhaps what is most striking about this account is how grateful the inmates were for the chance to eat some stale soup. Those who were not executed on arrival endured a living hell inside the camps. Some of them were undoubtedly my father's second and third cousins. If my great-grandparents had not emigrated to the United States from Poland, perhaps I would never have been born.

Rob Goldman tells of a prayer found next to a dead child in the Ravensbruck concentration camp. This child was one of ninety-two thousand victims there.

"O Lord, remember not only the men and women of good will, but also those of ill will. But do not only remember the suffering they have inflicted on us; remember the fruits we bought, thanks to this suffering: our comradeship, our loyalty, our humility, the courage, the generosity, the greatness of heart which has grown out of all this. And when they come to judgment, let all the fruits that we have borne be their forgiveness."[3]

Sadly, the suffering of holocaust victims cannot save their tormentors who did not repent. But the suffering of Christ tells us that he understands all our suffering, and the fruit of his pain is *our* forgiveness.

How does God respond to all this suffering? He yearns to end it all. One day, he will. John writes about this in Revelation 7:16-17:

> *"Never again will they hunger;*
>   *never again will they thirst.*
> *The sun will not beat upon them,*
>   *nor any scorching heat.*
> *For the Lamb at the center of the throne will be*
>   *their shepherd;*
>   *he will lead them to springs of living water.*
> *And God will wipe away every tear from their eyes."*

When we get to heaven, there will be no more suffering. No more crying. No more pain. When you suffer, understand this: God will one day wipe every tear away from your eyes. He wants to hold you and comfort you. He knows how you feel. He has seen it all. As you pray, let God wipe away the tears. He understands. "He heals the brokenhearted and binds up their wounds" (Psalm 147:3). Let him bind up yours.

---

[3]Rob Goldman, "Healing the World by Our Wounds," *The Other Side*, vol. 27, no. 6 (Nov./Dec. 1991), 24, as quoted by Richard J. Foster, *Prayer: Finding the Heart's True Home* (London: Hodder & Stoughton, Ltd., 1992), 238.

TAKING INVENTORY

1. What is your current view of suffering? How does it need to change?

2. What is your first reaction to suffering in your own life or in the lives of those around you? Are you more apt to run to God or to run away from him? Give some examples.

3. What lessons about gratitude have you learned from this chapter?

6

God Is Treasuring Me Like a Jewel

The nations will see your righteousness,
and all kings your glory;
you will be called by a new name
that the mouth of the Lord will bestow.
You will be a crown of splendor in the Lord's hand,
a royal diadem in the hand of your God.

Isaiah 62:2-3

What an amazing promise is given in this passage of Scripture! We are jewels in the hand of God. And not just any old, ordinary jewel; we are "a crown of splendor, a royal diadem" (Isaiah 62:3). He treasures us and we are extremely valuable to him. He holds us up in the air like the woman's lost coin, telling everyone, "Rejoice with me!" (Luke 15:9), just as Jesus told his disciples, "You are worth more than many sparrows" (Matthew 10:31).

Earthly Treasures

I remember choosing the engagement ring for my wife, Nadine. I went to a jeweler in Cagliari, Italy, on a road I walked down often as a child. There I saw it: the gold was twisted around a beautiful, small diamond. It was very small, but perfect. I looked at the ring in my hand, and I was bursting with love for my soon-to-be bride. I did not drop that ring. I did not lose that ring. I did not damage that ring. I treasured it.

Young people in love carve their names into trees or write them on walls to show their affection for each other. God says in Isaiah 49:16, "See, I have engraved you on the palms of my hands."

Parents invariably carry photographs of their children in their wallets. They never tire of showing these pictures to others—even complete strangers—because of their love for them and how much their children mean to them. How much more does God value us. He says in Isaiah 43:4—

> *Since you are precious and honored in my sight,*
> *   and because I love you,*
> *I will give men in exchange for you,*
> *   and people in exchange for your life.*

He gave his own son, Jesus, in exchange for us. Love like that is incredibly hard to fathom. I would find it extremely difficult to give up my son, Luke (or any of my children!), for my closest friends. It is unfathomable to think of giving him up for a stranger—or an enemy. But this is the story of the gospel:

> *For you know that it was not with perishable things such as silver or gold that you were redeemed from the empty way of life handed down to you from your forefathers, but with the precious blood of Christ, a lamb without blemish or defect. (1 Peter 1:18-19)*

Worth in the World

Sadly, the world doesn't always treasure us like jewels. We have all had experiences that made us feel worthless.

Some of us still feel worthless today. I remember going to MIT as a first-year student. I was far away from home. I missed my mom. I was scared. We had rush-orientation week, when all the freshmen had to be placed in housing. During that week, the various university fraternity houses hosted parties at which prospective recruits could meet the fraternity "brothers" and be evaluated.

On the first night, I went to one of those parties. There was music, beer and food. I talked for a few minutes with one of the brothers. He asked me what sports I played. I explained that I had played basketball, but I had given it up because I had to work to support my family. I told him that I was quite good at chess. He offered me a beer. I asked for a soda. He asked me what I liked to do. I said that I really wanted to study and get a good education.

Within a few minutes, I found myself in the lobby of the fraternity, sitting with another brother. He asked me, "So, what do you think of our fraternity?" I remember saying, "Oh, I like it. It's great. The people are friendly; I like the atmosphere." He started to explain, "You know, I really think APO might be a better place for you—we've called a car to take you there, to check it out."

I didn't get it. I said, "Well, really, I like *this* fraternity."

He looked at me and said, "You don't understand. We don't want you. You've been flushed."

At that moment, I became silent. I fought back the tears as I realized the implications of that statement. None of the fraternities took me that week. I do not think I tried too hard after the first one, though. I felt so worthless. I ended up in a great dormitory, Baker House, which eventually housed five undergraduate disciples of Jesus who changed my life. But to this day I can still recall how worthless I felt that night, riding away from the fraternity house.

Spiritual Worth

Have you ever felt that way? Have you ever failed an exam? Have you ever been "dumped" in a relationship? Have you overheard your father saying that "these children are nothing but aggravation"? Have you been called "stupid," "ugly," "slow" or "fat"? Let me tell you, God thinks differently about you. He is treasuring you like a jewel, just as Jesus treasured and had vision for his first century disciples. He saw the immoral Samaritan woman and saw a lady who could change a city (John 4). He saw demon-possessed Legion and saw a man who could change ten cities (Mark 5:1-20). He saw impetuous Peter and called him "the Rock" (Matthew 16:18). He saw James and John, and though they were impatient (Luke 9:52-56), he had vision for them to be men of power and called them the "Sons of Thunder" (Mark 3:17).

God sees you and me and calls us his sons and daughters, his ambassadors, sent out to change the world. It is time to get fired up about having a relationship with him. He is treasuring you and me like jewels!

TAKING INVENTORY

1. What is your most treasured earthly possession? (It doesn't have to be something spiritual.) Why do you consider it valuable?

2. Think about the time in your life when you felt the most worthless. How do you think God was feeling about you right then? What scripture can you use to back up your answer?

3. Thinking back to when you first became a Christian, what visionary nickname could Jesus have given you?

7

God Is Singing to Me

The Lord your God is with you,
*   he is mighty to save.*
He will take great delight in you,
*   he will quiet you with his love,*
*   he will rejoice over you with singing."*
*   Zephaniah 3:17*

This passage beautifully describes how we should feel as Christians. The Lord has taken away our punishment and has turned back our enemy, Satan. He is with us always (Matthew 28:20). He is mighty to save. He is rejoicing over us with singing.

I can still remember the day that my daughter, Hannah (now ten), was born in Bangalore, India. The hospital was very basic, with no electronic equipment. The delivery went well, and Nadine was resting that night. Little Hannah was dressed in fuzzy, light green pajamas. All night long I cradled Hannah in my arms, marveling at this little gem made by God, singing softly so that she would sleep. I will never forget that feeling. That is what God feels when he looks at us! The beautiful hymn often sung in our churches says,

Well, I hear God singing to me:
"Every nation must be saved!"
Well, I hear God singing to me:
"Every challenge must be braved!"
Oh, I feel God's Spirit in me:
Quench it not, too much at stake.
Well, I hear God singing to me:
Hear God sing for Jesus' sake.

Turning a Deaf Ear

Growing up, joy was not a feeling frequently experienced in my family. Four years after my dad left, when I was fourteen, my mother lost her job at the university. She was in her forties, and it was hard to find work. She felt much pain at the way her employer handled her dismissal. Money was scarce, and we had to struggle to make ends meet. My friends had cars and were involved in many extracurricular activities. We did not own a car, and I did not have the money to do many of the things that other teenagers were doing. The fun I did have was with a wild group of friends, and it was always associated with sin. There was a lot of shouting and unkindness at home, much of it coming from me. I decided that hard work was going to make my future different from that of my parents. It was hard for me to hear God singing at that time.

Joy Beyond Measure

The Bible paints a completely different picture of God than the one many of us grew up with. He is not stern and grumpy, just waiting for us to mess up so he can zap us. Rather, he is looking for an excuse to throw a party in heaven. He is the God who runs through the fields for us, crawls on his knees for us, throws open his arms for us, carries us in his arms and then throws a party when we get home! In all three parables in Luke 15, the shepherd, the woman and the father throw parties when they find what they lost. And Jesus said:

"In the same way, I tell you, there is rejoicing in the presence of the angels of God over one sinner who repents."
(Luke 15:10)

When Jesus entered Jerusalem, "the whole crowd of disciples began joyfully to praise God in loud voices." The Pharisees in the crowd told Jesus to silence his disciples, but Jesus said, "I tell you, if they keep quiet, the stones will cry out" (Luke 19:37-40).

God was joyful from the beginning. In his wisdom, he rejoiced in the creation:

"I was there when he set the heavens in place,
  when he marked out the horizon on the face of the deep,
when he established the clouds above
  and fixed securely the fountains of the deep,
when he gave the sea its boundary
  so the waters would not overstep his command,
and when he marked out the foundations of the earth.
  Then I was the craftsman at his side.
I was filled with delight day after day,
  rejoicing always in his presence,
rejoicing in his whole world
  and delighting in mankind." (Proverbs 8:27-31)

The Scriptures also describe nature as rejoicing in God's presence.

Let the sea resound, and everything in it,
  the world, and all who live in it.

Let the rivers clap their hands,
    let the mountains sing together for joy. (Psalm 98:7-8)

Isaiah frequently returned to the theme of nature rejoicing
in God's glory.

The desert and the parched land will be glad;
    the wilderness will rejoice and blossom.
Like the crocus, it will burst into bloom;
    it will rejoice greatly and shout for joy.
The glory of Lebanon will be given to it,
    the splendor of Carmel and Sharon;
they will see the glory of the Lord,
    the splendor of our God. (Isaiah 35:1-2; see also Isaiah
    44:23 and 49:13.)

Indeed, the followers of God are promised that nature will
rejoice in our presence:

You will go out in joy
    and be led forth in peace;
the mountains and hills
    will burst into song before you,
and all the trees of the field
    will clap their hands. (Isaiah 55:12)

Not only was God joyful in the beginning, but he
promises us joy at the end of time. Faithful servants in
Matthew 25:21-23 are invited to "Come and share your
master's happiness!" (Matthew 25:21, 23). The very nature
of heaven is to share the happiness of God for all of eternity!

The Joy of the Song

As an MIT student, I was initially unresponsive to the
gospel. I came to Bible discussion groups, and the lively

teaching and friendly people interested me. But I was consumed with my work. I felt that I had no time to travel across town to attend church. My viewpoint changed, however, in October of 1983.

I was busy preparing my master's degree thesis, and the Boston Church of Christ was hosting its annual World Missions Seminar. I attended the Saturday night presentation, which included a musical, almost operatic, performance of the song "I Will Be with You," performed by the Boston Freedom Singers. The song began with a deep-voiced man singing slowly and powerfully, "In the beginning, God made man to have fellowship with him." A woman's voice then sang passionately, quoting Psalm 8:4, "What is man that you are mindful of him, the son of man that you care for him?" As they sang, I began to weep, realizing that the infinite, eternal God cared about me, in spite of my insignificance on this earth. For the first time in my life, I could hear God singing, and I wanted to know this God.

Joyful Prayers

What should our response be to God's infinite joy? We need to rejoice in our prayers and in our lives as Christians. Joy is one of the fruits of the Spirit (Galatians 5:22). Though I had read that verse many times, I never fully realized that joy comes from God until my joyful friend, Mohan Nanjundan, pointed it out to me! I always thought that working hard was good and that joy was somehow associated with sin. These beliefs came from my own experience, in which all my laughter was tied to sin.

Our prayers need to be an outpouring of joy and thanksgiving before a joyful, singing God. He loves to hear us being happy. He wants us to have the attitude of the psalmist: "The Lord is my strength and my shield; my heart trusts in him, and I am helped. My heart leaps for joy and I will give thanks to him in song" (Psalm 28:7). We must remember, even in tough times, when God's hand is upon us, "For his anger lasts only a moment, but his favor lasts a lifetime; weeping may remain for a night, but rejoicing comes in the morning" (Psalm 30:5). He is singing. He is smiling. He is laughing. Let's hear God singing, and pray like we can hear him.

TAKING INVENTORY

1. *What was your view of God while you were growing up? How has that changed since you have met the God of the Bible?*

2. *Do you see Jesus as a joyful man? Find some passages that reflect his joy and write them down.*

3. *Do you have a favorite joyful song to sing to God in your quiet times? If not, will you find one and try it out today?*

8

God Is a Consuming Fire

Therefore, since we are receiving a kingdom that cannot be shaken, let us be thankful, and so worship God acceptably with reverence and awe, for our "God is a consuming fire."

Hebrews 12:29

The God we pray to is a God who welcomes us into his fellowship and forgives us completely of our sins through the blood of Jesus, and yet, he is also a God we need to fear. He wants us to be humble, to worship him with reverence and awe. He is a consuming fire, a jealous God who wants us to love him and not idols (Deuteronomy 4:24). God is

...the blessed and only Ruler, the King of kings and Lord of lords, who alone is immortal and who lives in unapproachable light, whom no one has seen or can see. To him be honor and might forever. Amen. (1 Timothy 6:15-16)

In Our Image

Our problem is that we think God is like us. In Psalm 50:21, God says, "You thought I was altogether like you." But God says, "My thoughts are not your thoughts, neither are your ways my ways" (Isaiah 55:8). Historically, societies which develop their own religions have gods that resemble humans. Greek mythology is full of sinful gods. Animism and Hinduism feature gods whose sins remind us of ourselves. But our Father in heaven is totally without blemish or stain, with a purifying holiness that is overwhelming.

You may have grown up in a household where compromise, deceit, broken promises and a lack of integrity were normal. A son of a prominent denominational minister in the United States was quoted as saying, "If God is like my father, I want nothing to do with Him."[1] You may view God in this way, too.

You may have been in the habit of trying to "get away with it" when it comes to sin and unrighteousness. Psalm 94:7 says that the wicked say, "The Lord does not see; the God of Jacob pays no heed." Jeremiah condemns the people of Israel: "They have lied about the Lord; they said, 'He will do nothing! No harm will come to us.'" (Jeremiah 5:12). As we pray, we must remember that our God is a consuming fire.

His Real Image

God appeared to Ezekiel in blazing fire in a vision by the Kebar river. The vision and the brilliant light amazed Ezekiel, and he fell facedown and listened to God (Ezekiel 1:27-28). Similarly, in Revelation 1, John saw Jesus in all his post-ascension glory. He was dressed in a robe with a golden sash around his chest (v13). His head and hair were white as snow, while "his eyes were like blazing fire" (v14). (Those eyes of blazing fire can see right through us, totally aware of all our sin.) His feet were like bronze glowing in a furnace (v15). A double-edged sword came out of his mouth, and his face was brilliant, like the sun (v16). Faced with the reality of Jesus, John fell at his feet as though dead. Jesus comforted

---

[1]Jerry Bridges, *The Joy of Fearing God* (Colorado Springs: Waterbrook Press, 1997), 218.

him and told him not to be afraid, but his first reaction was fear (v17). The paradox of God is this: though over and over again he tells us not to be afraid, he also says, "This is the one I esteem: he who is humble and contrite in spirit, and trembles at my word" (Isaiah 66:2). Also, Paul encouraged the Philippians to work out their salvation "with fear and trembling" (Philippians 2:12).

Peter was an ordinary fisherman, eager to learn from Jesus. But when he saw the power of God after a miraculous catch of fish, he begged Jesus, "Go away from me, Lord; I am a sinful man!" (Luke 5:8). Jesus told him, "Don't be afraid; from now on you will catch men" (Luke 5:10). When a holy God confronts us sinful humans, the only result can be fear and trembling. When Isaiah was first called by God, he had a vision that must serve as a model for us:

> In the year that King Uzziah died, I saw the Lord seated on a throne, high and exalted, and the train of his robe filled the temple. Above him were seraphs, each with six wings: With two wings they covered their faces, with two they covered their feet, and with two they were flying. And they were calling to one another:
>
> "Holy, holy, holy is the Lord Almighty;
> the whole earth is full of his glory."
>
> At the sound of their voices the doorposts and thresholds shook and the temple was filled with smoke.
> "Woe to me!" I cried. "I am ruined! For I am a man of unclean lips, and I live among a people of unclean lips, and my eyes have seen the King, the Lord Almighty."
> Then one of the seraphs flew to me with a live coal in his hand, which he had taken with tongs from the altar. With it he touched my mouth and said, "See, this has touched

your lips; your guilt is taken away and your sin atoned for."
Then I heard the voice of the Lord saying, "Whom shall
I send? And who will go for us?"
And I said, "Here am I. Send me!" (Isaiah 6:1-8)

Isaiah saw a vision of God's glory, but also of God's holiness (vv1-4). His first reaction was total brokenness. He realized that he and his people were deeply sinful in the presence of this holy God. And in that unworthy state, God extended his grace and forgave Isaiah (vv6-7). He then asked if Isaiah would go forth on his behalf (v8). It is very encouraging to know that God has forgiven us as Christians through Jesus Christ.

Our Humble Response

We must be totally aware of our own unworthiness. Job argued with God—and God's servants—until God spoke to him. Then Job said, "My ears had heard of you but now my eyes have seen you. Therefore I despise myself and repent in dust and ashes." (Job 42:5-6). This is the kind of reaction we should have when our sinful selves meet a pure, holy and perfect God.

David also understood our unworthiness in God's sight. After praising God, David prayed:

"But who am I, and who are my people, that we should be able to give as generously as this? Everything comes from you, and we have given you only what comes from your hand. We are aliens and strangers in your sight, as were all our forefathers. Our days on earth are like a shadow, without hope." (1 Chronicles 29:14-15)

He felt unworthy before the consuming holiness of God. Solomon asked God to hear men's prayers when they were made by someone "aware of the afflictions of his own heart, and spreading out his hands toward this temple" (1 Kings 8:38). Jesus rebuked the church in Laodicea, as they rejoiced in their material self-sufficiency, "You say, 'I am rich; I have acquired wealth and do not need a thing.' But you do not realize that you are wretched, pitiful, poor, blind and naked" (Revelation 3:17).

When I pray, I often pray the prayer of Revelation 3, "Lord, I am wretched, pitiful, poor, blind and naked. Please help me." Jesus commended the tax collector who prayed, "God, have mercy on me, a sinner" (Luke 18:13). Our material possessions or good deeds in no way make us worthy of coming into the presence of the holy one. It is by his grace alone that we can have a relationship with him. Let us never take that for granted.

Fearing God in Prayer

When we pray, let us give God the respect that he deserves. Yes, he wants to be our friend, but let us treat him as a true friend. Some of us pray using the name of God as a punctuation mark: "God, I just want to say, God, that you are great, God. And father God, you are awesome, God, and you help us, God, and you gave us Jesus, God. Thanks, God. Be with us, God." You get the point. Other times, our minds drift and wander, and we babble like the pagans (Matthew 6:7). Or we try to pray in a place that is too warm or too comfortable, and sleep comes upon us. Sometimes we dance with sin, and we wonder why God does not seem to listen to us.

A holy God requires us to be righteous, or he will not answer our prayers. In Psalm 66:16-20, the psalmist explained that he cried out to God, praising him. Yet, if he had cherished sin in his heart, even with all the prayers and loud cries, God would not have listened. God can reject our prayers if we do not do right.

In Joshua 7, the Israelites tried to attack Ai, but they failed (Joshua 7:1-5). God did not bless them because Achan took some of the devoted things at Jericho. Joshua tore his clothes and fell facedown before God, praying. But God's response was and is very instructive:

> The Lord said to Joshua, "Stand up! What are you doing down on your face? Israel has sinned; they have violated my covenant, which I commanded them to keep. They have taken some of the devoted things; they have stolen, they have lied, they have put them with their own possessions. That is why the Israelites cannot stand against their enemies; they turn their backs and run because they have been made liable to destruction. I will not be with you anymore unless you destroy whatever among you is devoted to destruction." (Joshua 7:10-12)

Similarly, in 2 Samuel 21, we read about a three-year famine during the reign of David. The people prayed, but God responded that the Israelites had violated their pledge to the Gibeonites by putting them to death (v2). This pledge was made in Joshua 9, hundreds of years earlier, but still God expected them to keep their word! Only after David made amends to the Gibeonites did God end the famine and answer prayer in Israel (2 Samuel 21:14). The prayer of *a righteous man* is powerful and effective.

I have had times in my Christian life when I have fasted, prayed, wept and begged God. But my sins (or the sins in my church) have stopped God from hearing my prayers. In Bangalore in 1990, we faced heavy persecution, and I prayed often, but I had no peace. I prayed, but I did not give my burdens to God (Philippians 4:6-7, 1 Peter 5:7). I was faithless and afraid, and bitter toward my persecutors. Sometimes I sat at home, my heart pounding with fear when the doorbell or phone rang. I wondered who it might be and what threats would be next. I walked down the street afraid to share my faith for fear that a policeman would see me. I became unkind to the people around me. The church went through a nine-month period of no growth, and it broke my heart. Only when I recognized my sins of fear, faithlessness and lack of joy did God again start answering my prayers. At other times I have struggled with distractions or unrighteousness, and I have found that I had few or no answered prayers in my life.

All the prayer in the world will not get through to God if it is not uttered from a pure heart. Remember, it is the prayer of *the righteous* that is powerful and effective. Our God is completely holy. He is a consuming fire, and his eyes pierce to the depths of our souls. Only when we strive to be holy, as he is holy, will our prayers be heard by him.

TAKING INVENTORY

1. How much do you value being in the courts of God's temple as you pray? Do you come before him with fear and trembling, reverence and awe? How do you view yourself before him—in good shape, because you have a job, and some money and a place to live? How will you change?

2. How focused on righteousness are you? Is the confession of sin a regular part of your life? Are you trying to pray through your problems when really there is sin to confess and be left behind?

3. Do you know of any disciples in your ministry whose sin may be holding back God's blessings? What will you do about it?

9

God Is More Powerful Than We Can Imagine

Now to him who is able to do immeasurably more than all we ask or imagine, according to his power that is at work within us, to him be glory in the church and in Christ Jesus throughout all generations, for ever and ever! Amen.

Ephesians 3:20-21

God runs. God crawls. God spreads out his arms. God carries us. He wipes away our tears. He treasures us like jewels. He sings to us. He is holy, burning like fire. And he is more powerful than we can imagine. Paul prayed that this incredibly powerful God would be glorified in the lives and hearts of the Ephesian Christians:

I pray also that the eyes of your heart may be enlightened in order that you may know the hope to which he has called you, the riches of his glorious inheritance in the saints, and his incomparably great power for us who believe. That power is like the working of his mighty strength which he exerted in Christ when he raised him from the dead and

seated him at his right hand in the heavenly realms.
(Ephesians 1:18-20)

The power that raised Jesus from the dead is available for us who believe. When we begin to understand how powerful God is, it will revolutionize our prayer lives.

Many of us serve a puny god—limited by our failures and experiences, by our disappointments and doubts. He is not the God of the Scriptures, but a tiny god of our own creation, to be manipulated rather than worshiped, ignored rather than obeyed. Maybe our earthly parents did not always come through for us. Maybe we have not seen all of our dreams come true. Despite these facts, the God of the Bible is more powerful than we can imagine.

Power over Creation

From Genesis to Revelation, the Bible resonates with the awesome power of God. The Bible begins with God's big bang, the creation. Verse after verse of Genesis explains God's incredible creation. He is bigger than the universe, and outside of it, too—as Solomon prayed, "The heavens, even the highest heavens, cannot contain you. How much less this temple I have built!" (2 Chronicles 6:18). Yet he "is not far from each one of us". (Acts 17:27). He is outside of time, as Moses prayed in Psalm 90:1-2.

God made everything we can see, and all we cannot see. He made all the stars. Some scientists tell us that if each were a grain of sand, they would cover the entire earth a foot deep. Yet each one has a name known to God (Psalm 147:4). He made the mountains and the weather; he created the solar system and all the galaxies. Yet he also "reveals his thoughts to man" (Amos 4:13). The prophet Nahum said, the "clouds are the dust of his feet" (Nahum 1:3). Not even a sparrow can fall to the ground without his knowing about it (Matthew 10:29).

God knows us completely. David said, "All my longings lie open before you, O Lord" (Psalm 38:9). David also said,

> *You know when I sit and when I rise;*
> *you perceive my thoughts from afar.*
> *You discern my going out and my lying down;*
> *you are familiar with all my ways.*
> *Before a word is on my tongue*
> *you know it completely, O Lord. (Psalm 139:2-4)*

We, however, cannot begin to understand God's immense power. He is more powerful than the greatest earthquake, the biggest fire, the most energetic explosion. Psalm 104:32 says of God, "he who looks at the earth, and it trembles, who touches the mountains, and they smoke." Human power is nothing in the face of God's awesome power. When Moses doubted God's power to feed his 600,000 men, God said, "Is the Lord's arm too short? You will now see whether or not what I say will come true for you" (Numbers 11:21-23). Hosea 10:7 describes Samaria and its king as being like a twig floating away on the surface of the waters. Faced with angry king Nebuchadnezzar's blazing furnace, Shadrach, Meshach, and Abednego declared,

> *"If we are thrown into the blazing furnace, the God we serve is able to save us from it, and he will rescue us from your hand, O king. But even if he does not, we want you to know, O king, that we will not serve your gods or worship the image of gold you have set up." (Daniel 3:17-18)*

Later these three men were rescued by an angel of God, who walked with them in the fire (Daniel 3:25, 28).

Isaiah the prophet "saw Jesus' glory and spoke about him" (John 12:41). He had a clear vision of God. He warned the palace administrator:

"Beware, the Lord is about to take firm hold of you
and hurl you away, O you mighty man.
He will roll you up tightly like a ball
and throw you into a large country.
There you will die
and there your splendid chariots will remain—
you disgrace to your master's house!"
(Isaiah 22:17-18)

Isaiah 40, quoted in the Gospels as being fulfilled by John the Baptist (Matthew 3:3, Mark 1:2, Luke 3:4-6), describes God's awesome power and man's insignificance. We are like grass that withers before the eternal God (Isaiah 40:7-8). James 4:14 says we are a mist. It says in Isaiah 40:12:

Who has measured the waters in the hollow of his hand,
or with the breadth of his hand marked off the
heavens?
Who has held the dust of the earth in a basket,
or weighed the mountains on the scales
and the hills in a balance?

Oceans fit in God's hand; the universe is several handbreadths to him; all the dust of the earth and the mountains fit in his basket. God is so big, so strong and so mighty! Isaiah 40:13-14 says that there is no one who can teach or instruct God—certainly not us! Isaiah 40:15 says, "surely the nations are like a drop in a bucket, they are regarded as dust on the scales." We can quiver and quake before worldly authorities. Yet in God's eyes, they are like a single drop in a bucket of water: insignificant. They are like dust on a measuring scale. As Jerry Bridges observed in *The Joy of Fearing God,*

The picture is of a pair of balance scales such as we might use in a science laboratory, and which in Bible times were used in ordinary commerce. We know that any dust on their trays would be immaterial, having no effect on the accuracy of measurement.

Imagine buying fruit and vegetables at your local supermarket, then telling the clerk at the checkout counter, "Please wipe the dust off the scales before weighing my produce—I don't want to pay for the dust." Such a concern is absurd. The weight of the dust is insignificant, irrelevant. And to God, the world's nations are nothing more than that.

It's not that the nations aren't imposing enough on a human level. Some of them down through history have been world empires. But however great they are or were, God is infinitely greater. Before Him all the most powerful states in all of history are no more than a drop in a bucket or dust on scales.[1]

God can exalt and bring down rulers simply by blowing on them (Isaiah 40:23-24; see also Psalm 75:6-7). He ensures that not a single star is missing (Isaiah 40:26). He is everlasting and the Creator. He does not get tired or weary like we do (Isaiah 40:28). Isaiah promised that if we hope in the Lord, we will renew our strength—walking, running and soaring with God (Isaiah 40:28-31).

Power Through Prayer

The awesome power of God is beyond our ability to describe or imagine. However, we can tap into this power through prayer, as Jesus said,

> "I tell you the truth, if anyone says to this mountain, 'Go, throw yourself into the sea,' and does not doubt in his heart

[1] Jerry Bridges, *The Joy of Fearing God*, (Colorado Springs: Waterbrook Press, 1997), 53-54.

*but believes that what he says will happen, it will be done
for him. Therefore I tell you, whatever you ask for in prayer,
believe that you have received it, and it will be yours."
(Mark 11:23-24)*

Our God can do more than we ask or imagine—he
promised to open doors for his servant Cyrus, the king
(Isaiah 45:1). He opened doors for Paul to preach (1
Corinthians 16:9, 2 Corinthians 2:12, Acts 14:27). Paul
asked the Colossians to pray for open doors (Colossians 4:3).
God gave the church in Philadelphia "an open door that no
one can shut" (Revelation 3:8). He promised Joshua, "I will
give you every place where you set your foot" (Joshua 1:3).

Power in Judgment

The Bible ends as it begins, with the awesome power of
God in judgment. In the book of Revelation it says,

*The seventh angel poured out his bowl into the air, and out
of the temple came a loud voice from the throne, saying, "It
is done!" Then there came flashes of lightning, rumblings,
peals of thunder and a severe earthquake. No earthquake
like it has ever occurred since man has been on earth, so
tremendous was the quake. (Revelation 16:17-18)*

There are rivers of blood (Revelation 14:20), hundred-
pound hailstones (Revelation 16:21), the mountains and
islands are leveled (Revelation 6:14, 16:20), and the sky rolls
away like a scroll (Revelation 6:14). Into this terrifying scene
of judgment, heaven opens up, and Jesus appears:

*I saw heaven standing open and there before me was a
white horse, whose rider is called Faithful and True. With justice he judges and makes war. His eyes are like blazing fire,
and on his head are many crowns. He has a name written*

on him that no one knows but he himself. He is dressed in a robe dipped in blood, and his name is the Word of God. The armies of heaven were following him, riding on white horses and dressed in fine linen, white and clean. Out of his mouth comes a sharp sword with which to strike down the nations. "He will rule them with an iron scepter." He treads the winepress of the fury of the wrath of God Almighty. On his robe and on his thigh he has this name written:

KING OF KINGS AND LORD OF LORDS. *(Revelation 19:11-16)*

This is not the wimpy Jesus sometimes portrayed in medieval and Renaissance art. This is a fierce, powerful son of God; we must fear him. But we also should each rejoice from the core of our being that this mighty, powerful Savior is on our side and will take us with him into glory one day.

I know one thing. When that great day occurs, I want to make sure that I, my family, my friends and everyone else are right with God. It is time for us to believe in this powerful God, to believe that he is with *us*. It is time to ask him to do things we have never dreamed or imagined. Our greatest troubles are small in the eyes of God. He is ready to do miracles; let us get ready to ask!

TAKING INVENTORY

1. *How do you currently view God? Think not in terms of quoting scriptures, but how does the way that you pray show your view of God?*

2. *What doors has God opened for you in the past? How about recently? What new doors will you ask to be opened as a result of reading this chapter?*

3. *How do you feel about the Judgement Day—really? Study out more scriptures that will cultivate a more Biblical view.*

10

God Is Preparing Us a Place

"Do not let your hearts be troubled. Trust in God; trust also in me. In my Father's house are many rooms; if it were not so, I would have told you. I am going there to prepare a place for you."

John 14:1-2

Jesus wants us to have peace in our hearts because he has prepared a place for us in heaven. God has a huge "house" with many rooms, for all kinds of people. There is enough space for you and me. Jesus wanted his disciples to remember where they were headed, because life on earth is much easier when you know where you are going in the end. Life, as a Christian, is like seeing a movie when you already know the ending—the good guys win! This should change the way we feel and the way we pray.

When Jesus prayed, heaven was in his mind. In Luke 10:17-20, the disciples came back after a successful ministry trip, rejoicing in the victories God had given. He told the disciples to rejoice, instead, because their names were written in heaven. In other words their final destination was more important than their day to day victories and defeats.

Jesus said, "Therefore do not worry about tomorrow, for tomorrow will worry about itself. Each day has enough trouble of its own" (Matthew 6:34). So often the troubles of today, rather than the glory of God, dominate our prayers. He wants us to remember that he is preparing a place for us in heaven. Heaven is so incredible that it is worth focusing our hearts on it frequently. During the great persecutions of the second half of the first century, God gave the Christians John's book of Revelation to remind them that they would win in the end. All the suffering was and is worth it, considering what heaven will be like.

Henry Kriete is a dear friend of mine, and one of my favorite preachers. When I first became a disciple, it was his teaching that moved my heart. He loves talking about heaven, and whenever I hear him, I want to go there. Let us examine some aspects of heaven, so we can be more motivated to pray with joy.

Hypocrisy Will Be Gone

Sometimes we see spiritual leaders fall, and it breaks our hearts. In addition we see our own shortcomings—but heaven is a place without sin. In Revelation 21, John described his vision of the new Jerusalem, heaven. Nothing impure, shameful or deceitful can enter it. Only those whose names are written in the Lamb's book of life will be there (Revelation 21:27). In this life we are being transformed into Jesus' likeness (2 Corinthians 3:17-18). But when he appears and takes us to heaven, "we shall be like him" (1 John 3:2). Our own weakness and sin will be gone, forever!

In this world we see hypocrisy too often. We see our political leaders say one thing and do another. In heaven things are totally different: hypocrisy does not exist. All relationships are transparent and pure. There is no shame. There is no need to wear masks. It is the kind of place where we would all like to go! And when we pray, we should pray as if we are already there. God knows our hearts, and we do not need to pretend or wear masks when we are with him. He loves us just the way we are.

Eternity with God

We also see in Revelation 21 that in the new Jerusalem, "the dwelling of God is with men, and he will live with them. They will be his people, and God himself will be with them and be their God" (Revelation 21:3). Revelation 7 describes a "great multitude" (v9) in heaven, who "are before the throne of God and serve him day and night in his temple" (v15). Jesus said, "Now this is eternal life: that they may know you, the only true God, and Jesus Christ, whom you have sent" (John 17:3). The Scriptures are clear: when we get to heaven, we will be in fellowship with God forever. It is a fellowship that we taste on earth when we pray. But on earth, "we see but a poor reflection as in a mirror; then we shall see face to face" (1 Corinthians 13:12).

We need to appreciate how awesome this eternal relationship with God will really be for us. In Revelation 21:9-10, the angel says to John,

> *"Come, I will show you the bride, the wife of the Lamb." And he carried me away in the Spirit to a mountain great and high, and showed me the Holy City, Jerusalem, coming down out of heaven from God.*

This wife is the church—us! Jesus marries us and is with us forever in heaven. I can still remember the sight of my bride, Nadine, as she walked down the aisle. The feeling of anticipation, unworthiness, and joy will be with me for the rest of my life. I was so glad she was coming to marry me! How much happier will we be to spend eternity in an intimate spiritual union with the Lamb.

Awesome Fellowship

Jesus painted a picture of heaven and hell in Luke 16:19-31. There we see Lazarus in fellowship with Abraham himself. In Luke 13:28-29, Jesus explained that Abraham, Isaac and Jacob, and all the prophets will be there in the kingdom of God on the Judgment Day. It will be like a feast, with people from everywhere in attendance. Hebrews 12:1 speaks about how we are surrounded by a "great cloud of witnesses." On the Mount of Transfiguration, Peter, James and John had a chance to fellowship with Jesus, Moses and Elijah (Matthew 17:1-9). This is what heaven will be like! Imagine having a chance to be with the prophet Samuel, or to spend time with Daniel—or Shadrach, Meshach and Abednego. How about having great fellowship with the apostle Paul or with Lydia, or a chance to meet the author of Hebrews! In this world when we do get to be with people we love and respect, often there is just not enough time, but in heaven that will never be a problem. The fellowship will be great and unending. It will be incredible!

Visions of Glory

When we pray, it is useful to imagine God sitting in heaven, in all his glory and majesty. In Revelation 4:1-2, John was taken through an open door in heaven, to the throne room of God. A rainbow encircled the throne (v3). There were twenty-four other thrones all around it, with the twenty-four elders (the twelve tribes of Israel and the twelve apostles) seated near God, dressed in white, with golden crowns (v4). Lightning and thunder came from the throne (v5). Before the throne was a sea of glass, clear as crystal (v6). The room was full of blazing light from the Holy Spirit (v5). Strange living creatures, covered with eyes, were continually praising God (vv6-8). At the same time, the twenty-four elders fell down and worshiped God, laying their crowns before him (vv10-11).

In Revelation 5, we see a slain Lamb (Jesus) approaching the throne of God (vv6-7). He was the only one worthy to open the scroll (vv4-5). When he took the scroll, all the living creatures and the twenty-four elders fell down before the Lamb (v8). They each had a harp, and "they were holding golden bowls full of incense, which are the prayers of the saints" (v8). They started singing (vv9-10), and one hundred million angels appeared, loudly singing about the Lamb (vv11-12). Then an even greater multitude sang in praise of the Lamb (v13). This vision is truly mind-blowing and glorious!

When we pray, our prayers are taken into this incredible scene. They are offered to the glorious Lamb before the throne of God—the only things in heaven made by human beings.

When we lived in India, we frequently went to Agra, to bring visitors to see the Taj Mahal, the beautiful mausoleum built to honor Shah Jahan's deceased wife. The marble, the intricate carving, the precious stones in the walls, the water in the forecourt and the symmetrical buildings all around combine to create a very inspiring, amazing sight. Yet this will be nothing compared to the glory of heaven. The New Jerusalem is described as being 10,000 times bigger in each dimension as the amazing Taj Mahal.

We have a church in Kathmandu, Nepal. Nearby are the Himalayas. We had a few leadership retreats for the Indian church leaders there. We stayed in the mountains, in lodges with no flushing toilets or running water. But though the physical amenities were not ideal, the view was unbelievable! The first morning, in the clear air, we could look straight up and see the snowy peaks. All I could say to God was, "Wow!" It was mind-boggling!

Each morning we went outside to have our quiet times on the mountainside. In the distance we could see Mount Everest, and on one side we could see Mount Amadablam, towering almost seven thousand meters (23,000 feet) above us. All around us were incredible peaks. Thousands of meters below we could see a small stream snaking between the mountains. As we prayed on the mountainside, clouds often enveloped us. It was a truly awe-inspiring sight! I sat and marveled at God's creation, thinking about how he had pinched the surface of the earth to make these mighty mountains. Imagine the vision we will have of the New Jerusalem, described in Revelation as about 1400 miles high!

Exciting Rewards

Heaven is a place full of blessings. Indeed, if God threw open the floodgates of heaven, so much blessing would flow out that we would not have room for it here on earth (Malachi 3:10). In the Sermon on the Mount in Matthew 5-7, Jesus referred several times to our reward in heaven. In 1 Corinthians 2:9-10 Paul was quoting from the Old Testament when he wrote, "No eye has seen, no ear has heard, no mind has conceived what God has prepared for those who love him." In context, Paul is referring to something we have now received as disciples that others before us could not conceive of, but there is a sense in which this passage will yet be fulfilled. God has plans to give us still more than we can imagine. Romans 8:32 says that, along with Jesus, God will "graciously give us all things."

How great is our reward in heaven? I do not know; I cannot comprehend it. I do know that on earth I have enjoyed the taste of wonderful food, the refreshment of a bath in warm water, the joy of swimming in clear water, the beauty of sexual union in marriage, the peace that comes with a good night's sleep and the happiness of knowing I have done a job well. Heaven will be far, far beyond any of these, which keeps me fired up when I pray!

No One Can Stop Us

Perhaps most exciting about heaven is that no one can stop us from going there—we can only stop ourselves. Heaven is worth any earthly price. Paul wrote, "I consider that our present sufferings are not worth comparing with the glory that will be revealed in us" (Romans 8:18). Romans 8:31-39 is a passage to remember when we pray. I quote it here in its entirety to remind us of God's incredible promises to us.

> *What, then, shall we say in response to this? If God is for us, who can be against us? He who did not spare his own Son, but gave him up for us all—how will he not also, along with him, graciously give us all things? Who will bring any charge against those whom God has chosen? It is God who justifies. Who is he that condemns? Christ Jesus, who died—more than that, who was raised to life—is at the right hand of God and is also interceding for us. Who shall separate us from the love of Christ? Shall trouble or hardship or persecution or famine or nakedness or danger or sword? As it is written:*
>
> *"For your sake we face death all day long;*
> *   we are considered as sheep to be slaughtered."*
>
> *No, in all these things we are more than conquerors through him who loved us. For I am convinced that neither death nor life, neither angels nor demons, neither the present nor the future, nor any powers, neither height nor depth, nor anything else in all creation, will be able to separate us from the love of God that is in Christ Jesus our Lord. (Romans 8:31-39)*

When I read this passage, I want to burst out the door and change the world! I want to pray and sing. When we pray, let us remember that we are praying to our Father, the one who has prepared an inheritance for his sons and daughters in heaven (Romans 8:17). He has prepared an incredible guest room, just for us. None of the problems of this life can stop us from making it to heaven. So, pray with great joy and faith to the God who is waiting to take us home to glory!

TAKING INVENTORY

1. *Think about some things in this life that cause you distress. Now think about the fact that nothing like this will exist in heaven.*

2. *Think back to what you would consider the most blissful or wonderful moments in your life. Now meditate on the fact that heaven will be far greater than these.*

3. *Do you think of God primarily as one who wants nothing more than to bless your life? How does that idea need to affect the decisions you make and the prayers you pray?*

11

Knowing God Through the Word

Now this is eternal life: that they may know you, the only true God, and Jesus Christ, whom you have sent.

John 17:3

By now, I pray that you have a better picture of who God is and how eager he is to be your friend. While reading what someone else writes about God is helpful, knowing God through your own study of the Bible is essential. Prayer is effective when we have the heart of Paul, who said, "I want to know Christ and the power of his resurrection" (Philippians 3:10).

We can get to know Christ, the living word of God (John 1:1), through the Bible, God's written Word. We will examine this more closely later, but the Scriptures show us how to pray, through the examples of great prayers recorded there. For example we see David's heart of prayer in the Psalms, and we see how Jesus prayed in the Gospels. But most importantly, we get to know God and his heart in the Scriptures. We fall in love with Jesus through the Scriptures. And when we are truly in love with God, our prayers are fresh and exciting.

In this chapter I want to share a few tips that have helped me to have refreshing and inspiring Bible study. I hope these suggestions help you in your study of God's word, motivate you to know God even better, and thus, enrich your prayer life.

The Spirit's Role

God wants us to know him and be close to him. For this reason he gave us the Counselor, the Holy Spirit, to live inside of us (John 14:16, Romans 8:9-16), fulfilling Jesus' promise to his disciples that he would not leave them as orphans (John 14:18). The Spirit is there to help us do what we want to do, which is to draw closer to God and to Jesus. When we read the Bible and when we pray, God's Spirit in us comes into contact with his Presence, and something very special happens. Invisible spiritual sparks fly as the Holy Spirit in us bonds us to the Almighty God!

The Spirit is always working to help us to have the mind of Christ (1 Corinthians 2:16), and he is grieved when we sin (Ephesians 4:30). The apostle Paul wrote that God's Spirit in us allows us to cry "*Abba*, Father" and that "the Spirit himself testifies with our spirit that we are God's children" (Romans 8:15-16). Later in Romans 8 Paul also said,

> *In the same way, the Spirit helps us in our weakness. We do not know what we ought to pray for, but the Spirit himself intercedes for us with groans that words cannot express. (Romans 8:26)*

The scripture commands us to "pray in the Holy Spirit" (Jude 20) and to "pray in the Spirit on all occasions" (Ephesians 6:18). What does this mean? I believe it means we must have spiritual prayers—alive and aware of God, not simply mouthing empty words or rituals. Our prayers are spiritual when they are deeply rooted in Scripture. Andrew Murray wrote powerfully about prayer. He observed,

> "Prayer and the Word of God are inseparable and should always go together.... Prayer is like fire. Fire can only burn brightly if it is supplied with good fuel. That fuel is God's Word which must be studied carefully and prayerfully."[1]

Living and Active?

For many of us our Bible study is dry and empty. It is just another ritual in our Christian life and we have lost hope for having vibrant, growing study times. I want to share with you about my own growth in this area, in the hope that it will help you to transform your own relationship with God.

As a young Christian, I loved the Word and sometimes read the Bible three hours a day in my quest to know God better. I remember in May 1984 reading almost the whole Bible in one month. I used highlighters to emphasize different themes in the Bible, and I made many notes in the margins. I had a good memory, and I was able to remember many verses word for word. But as I began to take on more and more leadership responsibilities in the church, my Bible study focused increasingly on preparing lessons, and less and less on feeding my relationship with God. Finally, in 1990 I decided to read through the whole Bible every year, and this helped me begin to have a better walk with God.

Though I read the entire Bible yearly, and I prayed daily without fail, I still did not always read the Word every single day. Many days would pass during which my only Bible study was done while teaching others or preparing lessons to teach. Sometimes I would read newspapers, magazines and books—but not the Bible. I would teach nonbelievers to

[1] Douglas Ed Cox and Edward A. Elliot, Sr., eds. *The Best of Andrew Murray on Prayer* (Uhrichsville, Ohio: Barbour Publishing, Inc., 1997).

read the Bible every day, and I would feel guilty that I was not really doing it myself. I often confessed this without actually changing—I felt justified in my heart because I read the Bible through every year (often twice a year), and I had memorized many Scriptures.

Finally, in February 1998 at a leadership conference in Los Angeles, I heard Kip McKean speaking about how we should love the word of God, and I realized it was time to change. I made the simple decision to read my Bible every day, at least one chapter, for the rest of my life. I have kept to that decision for the last eighteen months, and it is greatly encouraging. Earlier this year I read Sam Laing's excellent book, *Be Still, My Soul*, and learned about how he keeps a daily quiet time journal. So, six months ago I bought a little notebook, and every day I write down at least one (sometimes many) insights from the Scriptures. I had written down many insights through the years in the margins of my Bible, but I had not made it a daily discipline.

Therefore, from my own experience, let me give you five disciplines to having great Bible study, and then the ABCDs of great Bible study.

Bible Study Disciplines

Mark up your Bible. Use highlighters; write in the margins. Each color could represent a different theme. For example, blue might emphasize God's qualities; yellow might highlight passages about love; green about sin and righteousness; pink about prayer and faith; purple about joy; orange about evangelism and discipling; and magenta about the spiritual world (Satan, angels, demons, the Holy Spirit). You could circle every reference to God or Jesus or the Holy Spirit. It is clear that the early Christians who were fortunate enough to have Bibles wrote in the margins, and some of their comments were even mistaken by later copyists as being part of the original text. (Scholars can easily identify these variants, so the text we have is pure.)

Read the whole Bible every year. Focused study on individual books and passages is good, but it is important to have the broad picture of God's revelation deeply ingrained in our hearts. It can be helpful to read a different translation some years, to keep things fresh and interesting.

Read the Bible every day. Quoting Scripture, Jesus himself said, "Man does not live on bread alone, but on every word that comes from the mouth of God" (Matthew 4:4). In Old Testament times the Law required that the kings of Israel recopy the Law and read it all the days of their lives (Deuteronomy 17:18-20). The would-be Berean disciples were called noble because they examined the Scriptures every day (Acts 17:10-12). This also gives the Scriptures the opportunity to examine us every day!

Memorize key verses. Stuck to the head of our bed are many Post-It® notes, each one with a different verse my wife, Nadine, is memorizing. When we, as disciples, memorize Bible verses, it is easy to quote them to God in prayer, and it keeps us pursuing righteousness: "I have hidden your word in my heart that I might not sin against you" (Psalm 119:11). Proverbs 22:17-19 advises us to have the Proverbs ready on our lips, so our trust can be in the Lord.

Use a journal to record your insights every day. This will help you to consistently be fresh in your Bible study.

ABCDs

Once you are consistently reading the Scriptures, you can apply a few principles that I have found useful.

- *Ask questions of the text.* Who? Why? What happened? When? Where? How?

- *Be convicted.* What can I change? What can I learn here? Are there good/bad examples?
- *Compare the text with related passages.* Use a concordance. In the Old Testament, the prophets can be linked with historical books (Joshua, Judges, Ruth, 1 and 2 Samuel, 1 and 2 Kings, 1 and 2 Chronicles, Ezra, and Nehemiah). In the New Testament the letters can be cross-referenced with each other and with the book of Acts. The Gospels can be compared with each other. Revelation links well with Old Testament books like Daniel, Zechariah and Ezekiel.
- *Dream what it was like.* Read it carefully, and paint a picture in your mind.

An Example

Let's go through a passage using this approach. Read *Mark 6:32-44*, which is the story of Jesus feeding the five thousand.

A. Ask Questions of the Text
- Who? Jesus and his disciples, and many people.
- How? How did they get to Jesus? They ran (v33).
- What? They fed men (v44; this must have been ten to fifteen thousand people, including women and children).
- Why? It was too far for them to travel to get food, so Jesus did a miracle (v35).
- When? This was after John's death, at a time when Jesus might have been discouraged. Still, he was giving.
- Where? They were near water, but in a remote place (v35).

B. Be Convicted
- Jesus was so inspiring and giving that people ran to see him (v33). Am I that way? Do people want to be with me?

- Jesus did not feel tense with the crowd (v34). He had compassion on them, though John had just died. A good lesson for me!
- The disciples were too stingy to buy food for these guys (vv35-37). Am I like this? Indeed, sometimes I care more about money than people. I need to change.
- Jesus delegated the work to his disciples (v39). Am I doing too much myself? Am I delegating too much?
- He did not save the fish for himself (v41), but he shared with all! Am I selfish with treats of food or other things? Do I think of others first?
- He prayed for the food (v41). Do I thank God for all I have?
- They cleaned up afterward—no mess, no waste (v43). Here we can see that Jesus was generous in the amount of food he provided (enough for leftovers) and that he was not messy or wasteful. When guests come, am I generous? Is my house tidy?

C. Compare with Related Passages
Matthew 14:13-21
- He probably went there to mourn John's death (v13).
- He did not just teach; he also healed (v14).
- It says in verse 19 that Jesus directed the people to sit on the grass. But we know from Mark 6:39 that it was the disciples who sat the people down. We can see from this that sometimes Jesus directs people through his disciples. The word of Jesus may come to us through another disciple!

Luke 9:10-17
- The disciples also noticed that the people needed to find lodging (v12); this is not mentioned in Mark.
- Jesus specifically told them to have groups of fifty and

had the disciples sit everyone down (v14); in Mark it says they sat down in groups of hundreds and fifties, but it is not clear that this was Jesus' intention and plan.
- Everyone sat down (v15). It was peaceful—everyone obeyed!

John 6:1-13
- The reason the crowds followed was because they saw the miracles Jesus was doing (v2).
- It was a mountain where they were sitting (v3).
- It was near the time of the Jewish Passover feast (v4).
- They could see the crowd as it approached them (v5).
- Jesus was testing and teaching Philip at this time (vv5-6). This verse says that it was Jesus who first brought up the idea of feeding the people, and the disciples lacked faith in response to his question. In Mark 6:35-36, we only see the disciples' lack of faith, without Jesus' questions to Philip.
- Philip realized that eight months' wages was not enough to feed all these people (v7).
- Andrew found a boy with faith and food (vv8-9).
- There was "plenty of grass" (v10) in that place.
- They all ate as much as they needed (v11).
- Jesus said, "Let nothing be wasted" (v12).
- The loaves were made of barley (v13).

D. Dream What It Was Like
If you close your eyes, you can imagine a remote mountainside (Mark 6:35, John 6:3). There was plenty of beautiful green grass (Mark 6:39, John 6:10). It was springtime, so it must not have been too hot (near the Passover Feast, John 6:4). They were near the Sea of Galilee, so perhaps there was a fresh breeze there (Mark 6:32; John 6:1). They were probably tired from all the healing and teaching (Mark 6:31, 34). Suddenly they could see a great crowd

approaching, coming up the mountain (John 6:5). Jesus' immediate reaction was to meet their needs (John 6:5); the disciples' reaction was to send them away (Mark 6:35-36). He had a great conversation with Philip and the other brothers (John 6:6-8, Mark 6:35-38). Through a little boy, Jesus organized to feed them all (John 6:9). He got the disciples to sit them all down, peacefully (Mark 6:39-40). They ate enough to totally satisfy their hunger (John 6:11). The disciples then collected all the leftover pieces (John 6:12).

This ABCD method of Bible study, coupled with the practical tips mentioned above, has really helped me to have a fresh and exciting walk with God. God wants us to know him and to love him with all of our hearts. As we learn to pray in the Spirit—in accordance with his will—our hearts will be filled with joy, and we will be much more ready to face the challenges that await us in this world, primarily the challenge to touch other people with his love. We are not put on earth simply to enjoy our lives, but to know God and to help others to know God. We must learn to become prayer warriors, men and women who shake the world by our walk with God.

Our God is a God who can be moved by the prayers of men. He is willing to change his mind, if our entreaties are serious enough. He is willing to turn and have pity (Joel 2:13-14). When a nation repents, God is willing to relent and avert disaster (Jeremiah 18:8). When Moses stood in the breach between God and the Israelites, praying, God listened to Moses, and relented from destroying them (Deuteronomy 9:19, Exodus 32:11-14, Psalm 106:23). He turned away from his anger against Nineveh when the people repented and prayed in Jonah 3:6-10. Jesus was moved to do miracles when he saw the faith of people like the widow of Nain (Luke 7), the Canaanite woman (Matthew 15), and Mary and Martha (John 11). Spending time in the Scriptures and getting to know God as he is revealed there will produce such faith.

In the first half of this book I have deliberately taken time to help you focus on God. I am convinced that prayer can only be powerful when we clearly know who God is and believe he is the God who runs through the fields for us, crawls on his knees for us and does many other things to show us that we are treasures to him. Once we see God clearly and build a great friendship with him, prayer will come quite naturally.

We are ready now to move into some of the specifics of prayer. We will explore what moves the heart of God and how we can have prayers of impact. Notice how the first letter of each chapter title, taken together, spells "impact."

TAKING INVENTORY

1. *Is your Bible study fresh and exciting? Which of the Bible study disciplines listed in this chapter would specifically help you?*

2. *Do you use the Scriptures as you counsel and encourage other people, or just a lot of words and opinions?*

3. *Take a passage of Scripture and use the ABCD method to study it in your quiet time.*

PART 2

Prayers of Impact

12

Intimate Prayer

"Their leader will be one of their own;
their ruler will arise from among them.
I will bring him near and he will come close to me,
for who is he who will devote himself
to be close to me?"
declares the Lord.

Jeremiah 30:21

God looks for people who will devote themselves to being close to him. In other words he wants us to be his friends. In this kind of loving relationship with God, the heart of God is moved. Some of the greatest men of the Bible were described as God's friends, men who loved God with all their hearts.

Friends of God

Take Enoch, for example, who walked with God for three hundred years, and then God took him away (Genesis 5:22-24). Noah also walked with God (Genesis 6:9). Exodus 33:11 says:

> *The Lord would speak to Moses face to face, as a man speaks with his friend. Then Moses would return to the camp, but his young aide Joshua son of Nun did not leave the tent.*

Jehoshaphat and James—and even God himself (Isaiah 41:8)—all refer to Abraham as God's friend (2 Chronicles 20:7 and James 2:23).

Daniel 9 contains a magnificent, intimate prayer to God, the prayer of a friend. In Daniel 10:12, an angel told Daniel,

> *"Do not be afraid, Daniel. Since the first day that you set your mind to gain understanding and to humble yourself before your God, your words were heard, and I have come in response to them."*

Because Daniel was God's friend, God listened to him from the very first day he prayed!

In 1 Kings 8:59, Solomon ended his magnificent prayer by asking God,

> *"And may these words of mine, which I have prayed before the Lord, be near to the Lord our God day and night, that he may uphold the cause of his servant and the cause of his people Israel according to each day's need."*

God heard his prayer and answered him (1 Kings 9:3). God's heart is moved when he hears the intimate prayers of his friends.

Heartfelt Devotion

I understood God's desire for our friendship in a deeper way very recently. My seven-year-old son, Luke, and I were walking to McDonald's on our way to spend some time together. We had prayed together, and suddenly, he turned, looked up at me and said, "I love you, Dad." When he was born, I had said, "This is my son, whom I love; with him I am well pleased," quoting Matthew 17:5. But now I understood how God *felt* when he said this to Jesus—he was so happy to be receiving the spontaneous love of his Son. Those four words from my son are all I have ever wanted. They made me feel extremely happy. Surely such feelings come from God and are a mirror of what he feels when we love him deeply.

The book of Nehemiah is a rich account of one man's intimate friendship with God. In Nehemiah 1:4-11, we see a deep, love relationship between Nehemiah and God. In verse 5 he referred to God's "covenant of love" and his relationship "with those who love him." In verse 6 he pleaded, "let your ear be attentive." In verses 6-7, he said, "I confess"—a personal confession of sin. In verses 8-10 he reasoned with God, reminding him of his great deeds in the past. In verse 11 he appealed to God.

Continual Devotion

Nehemiah's prayer was that of an intimate friend of God. Nehemiah surely kept on praying for the following days, weeks and months. About four months later, God presented him with an opportunity to speak to the king.

In Nehemiah 2:1-8, we see that the king spoke to Nehemiah, asking him why he looked so sad (vv2-3). Nehemiah knew that this was his chance. So he quickly prayed one more time to God (v4), and he boldly spoke to the king about his problems. Miraculously, the king allowed him to go and rebuild his ancestral city (v6), and even sent letters with him to make things easier for him (v8). God heard his prayers because Nehemiah was God's intimate friend; he loved God, which moved God's heart.

In Nehemiah 2:18, when he met the people in Jerusalem, he challenged them to rebuild the walls, but he "also told them about the gracious hand of my God upon me."

Nehemiah wanted the officials to know that God, his friend, would help them.

I am going to get a little detailed here, but try to stay with me. There is something important we need to see. In Nehemiah 4, he faced opposition to his work. Verse 4 records his spontaneous prayer, "Hear us, O our God, for we are despised." When he faced more troubles in verse 9, he and the people prayed and posted a guard. In Nehemiah 4:14, he inspired the people by saying "Don't be afraid of them. Remember the Lord, who is great and awesome, and fight for your brothers, your sons and your daughters, your wives and your homes." Even his enemies knew God was with him (Nehemiah 4:15). In Nehemiah 4:20, he again promised, "Our God will fight for us!" Once more, in Nehemiah 5:19, he burst into spontaneous prayer, saying "Remember me with favor, O my God, for all I have done for these people." Nehemiah 6:9 and 6:14 record similar, intimate, spontaneous prayers, as do Nehemiah 13:14, 13:22, 13:29 and the last verse of the book, Nehemiah 13:31b. Nehemiah's relationship with God motivated him to do right. He could have enjoyed special privileges as the governor of Judah. But he refused the privileges, saying, "But out of reverence for God I did not act like that" (Nehemiah 5:15).

Nehemiah's intimate friendship with God had a deep impact on others, both inside and outside of God's kingdom. Nehemiah 9 records a prayer of the Levites trained by Nehemiah. There they praised God (vv5-6), recalled what God had done (vv7-31), appealed for help (v32), confessed their sins (vv33-37), and told God how they were feeling: "We are in great distress" (Nehemiah 9:37). In Chapter 12 we read how the Levites, under Nehemiah's direction, dedicated the wall with two large choirs, giving thanks to God. Nehemiah 12:43 says "The sound of rejoicing in Jerusalem could be heard far away." Chapter 13 records how Nehemiah dealt with sin by speaking of Solomon, who "was loved by his God, and God made him king over all Israel, but even he was led into sin by foreign women" (Nehemiah 13:26). Nehemiah obviously felt sad that though God loved Solomon, Solomon lost his friendship with God through his marriages to foreign women, and he wanted his people to avoid the same mistake.

Ultimately, because of Nehemiah's friendship with God, the walls of Jerusalem that had lain in ruins for about a hundred and fifty years were rebuilt in just fifty-two days (Nehemiah 6:15). The enemies of God's people were discouraged because they knew that this work had been done with God's help. The intimate prayers of one man had a huge impact in heaven and on earth!

When we are intimate with God, it also helps us to be close to our brothers. Because we are motivated to be close to God, we quickly resolve conflicts (Matthew 5:23-26). When God is our friend, we will talk to him about our friends on earth. Paul wrote in 1 Thessalonians 3:9-10,

> *How can we thank God enough for you in return for all the joy we have in the presence of our God because of you? Night and day we pray most earnestly that we may see you again and supply what is lacking in your faith.*

Paul's devotional times with God were filled with joy because of his brothers and sisters in Thessalonica. This must have encouraged them greatly when they heard it!

In Philippians 1:4 he told the church how much he always prayed with joy for them, and in Philippians 1:8 he said, "God can testify how I long for all of you with the affection of Christ Jesus." Imagine how they felt when they heard this! You know how encouraging it is for you when someone in the fellowship says, "I have been praying for you." Paul asked the disciples in Rome, "I urge you, brothers, by our Lord Jesus Christ and by the love of the Spirit, to join me in my struggle by praying to God for me" (Romans 15:30). His intimacy with God drew him near to other people.

How is your love for God today? Is it intimate? Do you make time to pray? In Luke 5:15-17, we read that Jesus withdrew often to be with God, and that God's power was present for him to heal the sick (v17). God's power is present when he is our friend and we communicate with him in that way.

Helping the Fallen

For me, each day I go on a prayer walk, and I talk to my friend, God. I praise him, and I bring before him my problems and spiritual dreams and goals. I try to live out Psalm 42:2 as I pray: "My soul thirsts for God, for the living God. When can I go and meet with God?" If I can steal away extra time to pray, or whisper a quick prayer, I try to do it. I need God.

And God keeps blessing my wife and me. He keeps bringing people to us who want to change their lives. In the three and a half years since we came to London, he has performed many miracles. Before arriving, we had prayed for God to lead us to people who had left him. We asked our friends about many people we had known who had left the Lord, one of whom was Freddie. Previously, the disciples had contacted him, but he was not interested in coming back. As we drove down the road one day, Nadine thought she saw him walking by. We stopped and searched for him and that very evening he came to church. A few weeks later, Freddie was restored.

A few months later, we asked God to give us evangelistic fruit as we entered a new year. For the first staff meeting of the year, our friends Fred and Emma Scott were the guest speakers. Normally we parked our car in a nearby parking lot, but for the first time, we parked beside a meter on the roadside that day. Fred spoke to the staff, and during his lesson I went out to feed the meter. As I returned, a young teacher was trying to get in at the door of the church office in order to go to the office above us. I spoke to her, and introduced her to my wife. She had just come to London and was looking for a church. A few weeks later Miandrea Steenekamp (now married to Cameron Williams) was baptized. Today she and her husband are doing great, and the Lord only knows what incredible plans he has for their future.

As that year drew to a close, I prayed for more people we had known to come back to Christ. The Lord put it on my heart to look in a ten-year-old directory for people's phone numbers. There was the work number of a lady we had frequently thought about, who had been a great Christian but had left the Lord many years before. I dialed her work number, and she was still working there! She was very happy to hear from us. A few months later, she was restored to Jesus Christ. A few months after that, Brenda transferred to a new job. God kept her in the same job all those years just so she could have a chance to come back to him!

Not long after this I went to Burger King one day to eat lunch. As is my custom, I invited the people serving us. The woman who served us was very friendly. The sisters followed-up with her and built a friendship, even though she could not come to any meetings of the church due to her busy work schedule. She did, however, see her need for God, and in March, she was baptized into Christ. Though later she left the Lord, she is now in the process of coming back to Christ.

That same month I went out and prayed to meet some-one that day who would become a Christian. As we walked along the road, my friend Jeff and I stopped a man on a bicycle, and he and his wife later became disciples.

That summer, my wife Nadine was traveling to Manchester by train. She had heard about others sharing their faith on intercity trains, and meeting people who were interested in God. So she prayed for God to lead her to someone who was seeking him. On the train, she sat next to a lady, Dr. Marelize Vorster. She invited Marelize, who was quite interested. The sisters in Manchester also independently invited Marelize. A few weeks later, she was baptized into Christ. She now leads the teen women in the London Church of Christ.

Running the Race

In 1998, I planned to run in the London marathon. I had prayed consistently for God to help me to finish, but I did not ask him to use the race to bring someone to him. The day before the marathon, I was praying, and I realized my lack of faith. I apologized to God and asked him to help me meet someone who would become a disciple. The day before the marathon, I went to Cameron and Miandrea's wedding. Passing by the wedding was a man wearing a marathon shirt, so I invited him to church. He gave me his phone number, saying he would like to come some time, but he never did. But I knew that God would bless me if I kept praying and believing—he is my friend; he will not let me down.

On the day of the race I spoke to a number of people, the last one on my way home—I was extremely tired! On the bus a man noticed that I had run in the marathon, and he started speaking to me. His name was Gary Clark, and he was training to be a solicitor (lawyer). After much prayer and many phone calls, he finally came to church. I never gave up on him, because I was sure that God had answered my marathon prayer, and he was the only one left who had not rejected the gospel. Finally, after seven months, Gary was baptized into Christ. He has now finished law school and is doing great as a disciple.

A Child's Prayers

One spring day, Nadine went to a park with the children. She saw a young lady on the other side of the park, and the Holy Spirit prompted her to go and invite her. The woman, Lisa, was friendly and came to church. But after a few weeks, she stopped coming, although we had prayed for her as a family quite frequently. Our son, Luke, kept praying for her, long after we had given up and she had stopped coming to church. After a year she came back to church and was baptized!

An Unexpected Response

About a year prior to this writing, I was pouring out my heart, trying to help a weak Christian stay faithful. I was sitting in the cafeteria of University College, London, speaking quite loudly. A man heard us and asked, "Can I join you?" My friend ended up leaving Christ, but this man came to my house, studied the Bible and started coming to church. Now John Perez is a disciple and a future ministry staff intern in the London church. His roommate at the time was named Martin, and I also had a chance to invite him. After visiting the church in London, he is now back in the United States, attending the church in Denver. He is studying the Bible with the brothers there.

Just a few months later we were praying and sharing our faith for the Men's Forum in London. I prayed that God would lead us to someone that day who would be open to Jesus. We met a mother and her teenage son. The next day my daughter Hannah and I visited their home. There we met her daughter, who was baptized recently.

A Family Victory

My wife had a troubled relationship with her dad while growing up. From the day she was baptized, Nadine prayed every day for her parents to be saved. After she had been a Christian just over a year, in January 1985, her mother, Any Descotes, was baptized. A year and a half later, her brother Franck was baptized. He and his wife, Fabienne, now lead the Paris Church of Christ. Their father, Gerard, was not as receptive to the gospel, but Nadine kept praying. Gerard faced many challenges in his life, but he still did not repent. We all kept on praying. He lost his job. We prayed. He was diagnosed with cancer. We prayed for healing and salvation. After sixteen long years Franck and I baptized Gerard Descotes into Christ in Paris. God hears the prayers of his intimate friends!

Finally, just a few weeks before I wrote this chapter, I was on my way for a short stay in the United States. The church was having a month in which we were praying for everyone we knew to be saved. At the airport, the lady who asked me the security questions was very friendly. So I asked her about her life and about her relationship with God. I put her in touch with some of the sisters. A few days later, we had a leaders' meeting. I held up the list of my friends whom I was praying for, and I announced that by faith God would help at least one of them to become a Christian soon. I prayed for all of them. I prayed for Leoni every day. And eight weeks later, at the end of October, Leoni Cortez became a Christian. God did not save her because I am a good guy, or because she is a good woman. He saved her by his grace. But I do believe that God is my friend, and I am his friend—and he listens to my prayers.

A Mother's Prayer

Several years ago, Michelle Matthews was baptized into Christ, starting her new life of following Jesus. However, what happened next was shocking. The day after her baptism, she went to a church-wide service of the London Church of Christ. In the fellowship someone asked to hold her nine-month-old son, Nathan. Michelle did not know who the person was, but assumed it was a Christian from another geographical sector of the church. Not wanting to be unfriendly now that she was a new disciple, she gave her boy to the woman to hold.

During the crowded fellowship time, the woman made her way out of the building, taking baby Nathan with her. In the crush it took a few minutes for Michelle to notice that the woman and her son were no longer around. She asked some of the sisters from her sector to help her search the Apollo Theatre, after which an announcement was made that her baby had disappeared. Hundreds of us gathered together in fervent prayer to God. We then called the police, and they put out an announcement to London Transport and to police in the local area to be on the lookout for a woman and a child.

Michelle sat in the police station, waiting and praying. While Michelle prayed, God was working. Soon after the announcement was relayed to London train and bus drivers, Nathan and the woman boarded a bus several miles away. The driver noticed that the woman was white, while the baby was black and in distress. He called back to his depot, and they alerted the police, who came and picked up the lady on the bus. Shortly afterward, after five hours of desperate prayer, Michelle was reunited with her baby.

Three years later, they both are doing well. Michelle is a strong, faithful disciple. She has led others to the Lord. She leads a group of women and even oversees the single mothers' ministry in the East section of the London church's ministry. Michelle knows what it means to be intimate with God! She recalls,

> Waiting in the police station for information concerning my son was the most intense time of my life. I remember praying fervently for God to bring Nathan back to me. I also remember thinking that I might never see him again, especially as the minutes turned to hours, and that maybe God was trying to teach me as a one-day-old Christian that he needed to be enough for me. Eventually, I prayed that God would help me to totally surrender to his will and that even if I never saw my baby alive again, I would still stay faithful as a Christian and never fall away.
>
> It took me a long time to get to the point where I really meant that prayer—in fact, it took five hours. But immediately after I reached the point when I felt totally surrendered, the police officer came in with the news: "We've found your son!"
>
> Since that time, whenever I've struggled in my faith, I always look back to that moment and renew my commitment to God. That low point of my new life as a Christian has turned into the strongest reference point of my spiritual life.

I am certain that God was pleased by Michelle's honest heart in her prayers and her spirit of surrender. She was intimate with God. She delighted herself in the Lord, and he gave her the desires of her heart (Psalm 37:4).

Friendship and Sacrifice

We all have close friends. For intimate friends, all of us would be ready to make sacrifices, to go out of our way to help them. I am not a great guy, but I feel like God goes out of his way to help me. I like to think that he does it because he is my friend. Let's become more intimate in our prayers and see miracles like never before!

TAKING INVENTORY

1. *What good reasons do you have to think of God as your intimate friend?*

2. *How should thinking that way change the way that you pray?*

3. *How do the stories of answered prayers in this chapter affect your faith and the way that you want to pray?*

13

Mighty Prayer

*I tell you the truth, anyone who has faith in me will do
what I have been doing. He will do even greater things
than these, because I am going to the Father. And I will
do whatever you ask in my name, so that the Son may
bring glory to the Father. You may ask me for anything
in my name, and I will do it.*

John 14:12-14

Jesus, in this passage, began by explaining that his
followers will do what he had been doing. They will live to
bring glory to God and to reconcile men to their Father in
heaven. He promised that those with faith in him can do
even greater things than he accomplished, through the
power of prayer. Our mighty God wants mighty things to
happen on earth—especially in his church, as we do what
Jesus did.

In his famous book on prayer, William Law wrote that
prayer is a tool "not for getting man's will done in heaven"
but "for getting God's will done on earth."[1] The nineteenth
century British missionary William Carey said, "Attempt
great things for God; expect great things from God." In Psalm

---

[1]William Law, *The Spirit of Prayer and the Spirit of Love,* ed. Sidney Spencer
(Canterbury: Clarke, 1969), 120.

81:10, God says, "Open wide your mouth, and I will fill it."
In other words, the more we expect, the more he will give! As
the great preacher Charles Spurgeon said,

> "Thou mayest expect great things from him who made
> the heavens and the earth. Look up at the stars, and see how
> the Lord flung them about by handfuls; and remember that
> all the stars that are visible to you are only the sweepings of
> star-dust by the door of God's great house."[2]

God knows what we need before we ask him (Matthew
6:8). In Isaiah 65:24, God promises, "Before they call I will
answer; while they are still speaking I will hear." Even *before*
we pray, God is getting ready to answer us! Jesus promised
in Mark 11:23-24 that he who believes and prays can move
mountains. It is time for us to have mighty faith and prayers
and to expect mighty things from our mighty God.

Mighty Work

Mighty prayers involve mighty work. In Joshua 10:1-14, the
Gibeonites were under threat from the Amorite armies. They
were overwhelmed, and they begged for help (v6). After
Joshua heard from God that he should go (v8), he under-
took an all-night march to save the Gibeonites (v9). Why did
God speak to Joshua? Most likely, Joshua had learned from
the mistakes he had made earlier: in chapter 9, he believed
the Gibeonites' story after sampling their provisions, but he
did not inquire of the Lord (Joshua 9:14). This time, he was
determined to depend on God. So he asked God if they
should go. And God said, "Do not be afraid of them; I have
given them into your hand" (Joshua 10:8). After the all-
night march, God moved powerfully, throwing the Amorite

[2]C. H. Spurgeon, *Encouragements to Prayer*, sermon on July 9, 1888 (London: Passmore & Alabaster, 1894), 460.

kings into confusion (v10). As they retreated, huge hail-stones fell from the sky (v11), killing more Amorites than the Israelites had killed with the sword.

Mighty Specific

Mighty prayers are specific. On that same day, Joshua offered up a mighty, faithful prayer. He spoke to God about the sun and moon, asking them to stand still until Israel could win the victory (vv12-13). Indeed, though verse 12 says that Joshua spoke to the Lord, in his prayer he appears to be directly addressing the sun and moon, telling them what to do. This was mighty faith! And God stopped the sun and moon for about a full day: "There has never been a day like it before or since, a day when the Lord listened to a man. Surely the Lord was fighting for Israel!" (Joshua 10:14). Joshua asked with total faith. He knew he was a son of God and that he could ask for anything he wanted (Matthew 7:7-11). He would have looked extremely foolish if God had not answered his request. But God knew that Joshua believed, and he answered his prayer.

In Luke 18:35-43 we read about a blind beggar who heard that Jesus was passing by. He knew what he wanted. He asked Jesus to help him. Everyone told him to be quiet. But he kept on asking, believing Jesus would hear him. And when Jesus asked him what he needed, he responded boldly, pleading for his sight. And he got it! Mighty faith is specific in its requests, bold in its attitude and waits in expectation for God's reply.

David said in Psalm 5:3 that he would daily lay his requests before God, and "[I] wait in expectation." In the middle of the genealogies in 1 Chronicles, we read that

Jabez cried out to the God of Israel, "Oh, that you would bless me and enlarge my territory! Let your hand be with me, and

keep me from harm so that I will be free from pain." And God granted his request. (1 Chronicles 4:10)

He was specific; he cried out; God answered! How sad it is that many of our prayers are "Lord, be with so-and-so; God help so-and-so...." But *we are not specific*. Specific prayers are faithful prayers, mighty in power.

When we really believe, we will be ready to act in order to see the answers to our prayers. We will go through life with eyes open, looking for our Father's answers to our pleas. Abraham believed God, it says in James, and "his faith and his actions were working together, and his faith was made complete by what he did" (James 2:22). God performed a mighty miracle in Abraham's life because he had mighty prayers of faith.

Mighty Victory

Ugo is a Christian in the east sector of the London Church of Christ. He is very intense and serious in whatever he undertakes and is a great student of the Bible. Yet in five years and eight months of Christian life, he had never led anyone personally to the Lord. He had tried and prayed many times. A group of brothers met together to talk about their spiritual lives, and they encouraged him to be specific in prayer about bearing fruit for God. Ugo was honest, confessing that he had thoughts like, "God doesn't want me to be fruitful." Nevertheless, Ugo took up the challenge of being fruitful that very month.

Ugo prayed specifically and repeatedly, begging God for a soul. God heard Ugo's prayers as he resolutely followed up on people whom he had already invited to church, reminding them to come. One of these people was Yomi, a man who lived in Birmingham. Yomi went to the Birmingham church because of Ugo's encouragement, and on a great day in

September, he was baptized into Christ! Like Joshua and his men, Ugo's specific prayers were matched with action that allowed God to answer his requests.

Mighty Faith

When she was twenty-five years old, Linda Hender was convinced that she was going to die. One week, these feelings were particularly strong. She decided to go in to work, rather than stay at home. Because she lived with her parents, she was afraid that if she stayed at home, her parents might be killed as well. She wrote a note to her parents, which she placed under a pillow, explaining what to do in the event of her death. That week, she decided to stay in her office, where she worked as an animator, for as long as possible, since she considered it safe there. During lunchtime one day, she decided to go to a cashpoint (ATM) machine to withdraw some money. Incredibly, as she walked to the bank, a spade fell off some scaffolding at a building site onto her head, smashing open her skull. At the hospital, the doctors told her parents that she had twenty minutes at most to live. She was in a coma, unable to see or move.

After several days, Linda started to regain consciousness, but was unable to move or speak. At this time she prayed to God—a simple, faithful prayer—that he would rescue her. Remarkably, she made an almost complete recovery, despite having a large steel plate inserted into her skull. Even though she was not yet a true Christian, God heard her mighty prayer. (God has often heard and answered the prayers of non-covenant and even very sinful people: see 1 Kings 8:41-43; 2 Chronicles 33:12-13; Jonah 3:8-10 and Acts 10:1-4).

Linda decided to start seriously seeking God. She went to a local church. Despite being unhappy there, she saw no better alternative and attended that church for over a decade. During this time, she got married and had two children. But she was still not happy in her relationship with God—she knew something was missing.

In early 1997 she was invited to a Women's Day program by Geraldine Kendall (a women's ministry leader in London, seven months pregnant at the time) and Angela Broughton. The night before, these women had prayed all night, begging God to lead them that next day to people who were seeking him. Exhausted after the all-night prayer, Geraldine nevertheless went out to meet people, convinced that God would lead her to someone who was seeking the truth.

Geraldine's mighty prayer and mighty work moved the heart of God. Linda met her on the road a few hours later! She came to the Women's Day program and loved it. She started studying the Bible with the sisters, and several weeks later, she was baptized into Christ. Linda now totally understands why God answered her prayer for survival from her freak accident years ago and wants to help as many people as possible become Christians.

Linda is faithful to this day and is one of the most joyful, serving Christians in the northwest sector of the London church. She makes refreshments for the church soccer team and is very generous. She also performs regularly at church events, using her singing talent for the Lord. She knows that mighty faith in a mighty God brings mighty miracles!

Like Geraldine, Unni had mighty faith. He is a brother in the Cochin Church of Christ in Kerala, India. He has a sister, Shanti, who was totally discouraged about her life. She was pregnant, unmarried and rejected by her family. She had decided to end her life, but Unni did not lose his faith in God. He prayed faithfully for her every day. He invited her to church many times, and she finally visited. Other disciples got involved in her life, and she became a disciple soon after that.

After becoming a disciple, Shanti's life totally changed. Her depression ended, and she became joyful and happy. She gave birth to a lovely boy she named Abednego. God blessed her life with a job with HOPE Worldwide in New Delhi, and God has even blessed her with a fine young man, Ruben, who wants to marry her. All because her brother, Unni, believed that Shanti could change. He prayed with mighty faith and acted on that faith, believing his prayer would be answered.

Another story of mighty faith and prayers comes out of India. Stella and her husband, Johnson, went on the mission team to Hyderabad, India. One day while riding a bus, Stella met a young lady I will call Eva (not her real name). This woman told Stella she used to attend the London Church of Christ, and that she was visiting Hyderabad for a couple of days to take an exam, after which she would be going back to another part of India. She expressed some interest in coming to the church, but then suddenly the bus stopped and she got off, and Stella never got her number. Distraught, Stella went home and begged God that she would see Eva again the next day, despite the fact that Hyderabad is a city of four million people. Sure enough, the next day, in a different part of town, Stella and Eva ran into each other again. Eva went to the church in Bangalore and was subsequently baptized there. Five years later, she is happily married, and she and her husband play a key role in one of the congregations in the Middle East.

Even More Mighty Faith

Pam, Roger and George Mathew all became disciples in the great Chicago Church of Christ. Being from an Indian background, each of them decided to go back to India to preach the word of God. They had always prayed that God would open a door for their family to be saved. Their family, however, lived in Kottayam, India, a small backwater town of about 100,000 people—in a nation of fifty cities of nearly a million people and hundreds of cities larger than Kottayam.

By the grace of God, as the three prayed, a church was planted sixty miles from Kottayam in the city of Cochin. They kept praying and preaching. The next year, one of the brothers in Cochin, Santosh Kagu, had a job offer out of town. The place: Kottayam! By faith, he took the job and moved there with his wife, Nalini, and the two of them started a family group. One by one souls were added, until a year later, there were sixteen disciples in Kottayam. At this time, the Mathew family's prayers intensified. A ministry staff couple was sent to lead the church, and Kottayam became an independent church planting. (It has grown to one hundred members since that time.)

The Matthews' grandfather, T.A. Varkey, was one of the most influential figures in the family and also in his community. He had been very proud toward the church, concerned that his grandchildren had joined a religious cult of some kind during their studies in America. He did, however, visit the church in Bangalore, and the trio continued to pray for him.

When the church was planted in Kottayam, Mr. Varkey visited, but still he did not change. The Christians prayed for God to move powerfully in his life. His health began to decline, and then he had a stroke. Pam, Roger and George started fasting weekly for him. Mr. Varkey agreed to study the Bible and realized he needed to become a Christian. Roger traveled from Bangalore to Kottayam to baptize him, but the rest of the family and his neighbors gathered and threw the brothers out of the house before they could baptize him. Mr. Varkey was afraid. His condition worsened and he had a second stroke, paralyzing half his body. But his grandchildren kept on praying mighty prayers of faith, and they acted on their prayers.

George was living in Cochin and traveled twice a month to Kottayam to study with his grandfather, even though he was no longer receptive to the truth. The whole Bangalore church of six hundred disciples prayed for him. After many more studies, he again decided to be baptized.

George went to the house. He prayed and shut the door behind him. Mr. Varkey begged to be baptized. George prayed and remembered how Jesus had closed the door to keep out the faithless people when he healed Jairus' daughter in Mark 5:36-43. So, George locked the door, filled up the bathtub and prepared to baptize his happy grandfather. Outside, the family realized what was happening. They heard the sound of running water inside, and they were furious. They tried to break down the door. They tried to call the police to stop the baptism, but the phone was dead. Soon, it was too late. Of his own free will, Mr. Varkey was baptized into Christ. George opened the door, and the neighbors and relatives came in to see Varkey, smiling and wet. Two weeks later he died and went to be with God.

Faithfully, Pam, George and Roger prayed specifically for Kottayam to have a church and for their grandfather to be saved. But they also, like Joshua, were prepared to act on their prayers. When it was time to preach in India, they went. When it was time to study with Mr. Varkey, they went. And when it was time to be bold and to save a soul, they risked their reputations so that a man could have his sins forgiven. *Mighty* prayers of faith move the heart of God to do mighty miracles!

A Mighty God

The God who can do more than we ask or imagine is ready to answer our prayers! He parted the Red Sea, stopped the sun, slew entire armies, healed the blind and even raised the dead when his children requested it. He is ready to do miracles in our lives. His heart is moved when we tell him what we want. When we believe and act, he will answer us! Let us pray specific, faithful prayers to our awesome, mighty God.

TAKING INVENTORY

1. *Why do you believe that you can become known as a person who prays mighty prayers?*

2. *Why does it make sense that God would want your prayers to be mighty?*

3. *Which quality described in this chapter do you need to most focus on to enjoy the power of mighty prayer?*

14

Praise and Thanksgiving

For long ago, in the days of David and Asaph, there had been directors for the singers and for the songs of praise and thanksgiving to God.

Nehemiah 12:46

Praise and thanksgiving are a natural part of prayer. We all want to praise the ones we love, but in life, we often take each other for granted. We get used to saying little to encourage others. We do not thank them either, and this pattern can creep into our prayer lives. We can use God to meet our needs, but fail to glorify him as our God. We cannot fathom how much it means to God when his children appreciate him.

Reading and praying through the Psalms is a great way to learn to praise and thank God in prayer. David said,

> *I will exalt you, my God the King;*
> *I will praise your name for ever and ever.*
> *Every day I will praise you*
> *and extol your name for ever and ever.*
> *(Psalm 145:1-2)*

I will praise the Lord all my life;
I will sing praise to my God as long as I live. (Psalm 146:2)

The great reformer Martin Luther loved "the juice, the strength, the passion, the fire which I find in the Psalter."[1] Richard Foster notes that "in the early Christian communities it was not unusual to memorize 'the entire David.' …Jerome said that in his day one would frequently hear Psalms being sung in the fields and gardens."[2]

Hand in Hand

What is the difference between praise and thanksgiving? Praise appreciates God for who he is, while thanksgiving appreciates God for what he has done for us. But they are hard to separate. In many of the great prayers of the Bible, they go together (1 Chronicles 29:10-14, Psalm 100:4-5, Revelation 11:17-18). In his excellent book, *The Joy of Fearing God*, Jerry Bridges observed, "It's difficult to separate thanksgiving from praise in our worship of God. A better practice is to join them, as we see in Psalm 100."[3]

Enter his gates with thanksgiving
and his courts with praise;
give thanks to him and praise his name.
For the Lord is good and his love endures forever;
his faithfulness continues through all generations.

God loves to be worshiped, and he loves to be thanked. Once again, to quote Foster,

---

[1]As quoted in Dietrich Bonhoeffer, *The Psalms: the Prayer Book of the Bible*, translated by James H. Burtness (Minneapolis: Augsburg, 1974), 25.

[2]Richard J. Foster, *Prayer: Finding the Heart's True Home*, (London: Hodder & Stoughton, Ltd., 1992), 116.

[3]Jerry Bridges, *The Joy of Fearing God* (Colorado Springs: Waterbrook Press, 1997), 239.

Our God is not made of stone. His heart is the most sensitive and tender of all. No act goes unnoticed, no matter how insignificant or small. A cup of cold water is enough to put tears in the eye of God. Like the proud mother who is thrilled to receive a wilted bouquet of dandelions from her child, so God celebrates our feeble expressions of gratitude.

Think of Jesus healing the ten lepers. Only one returned to give thanks, and he a Samaritan. How moved Jesus was by the one, how saddened by the nine! Think of the woman who bathed her Master's feet with the tears of gratitude. How stirred he was by her simple devotion! Think of the woman who in outlandish waste anointed Jesus' head with costly perfume. How touched he was by this lavish act of adoration! And what about us? Dare we hold back? It brings joy to the heart of God when we grip that pierced hand and say simply and profoundly, "Thank you, bless you, praise you."[4]

In 2 Chronicles 20:1-13, king Jehoshaphat of Judah learns that a vast army of Moabites and Ammonites are about to attack him. He had been a godly man for many years (2 Chronicles 17:3-4), and so his first instinct was to depend on God (2 Chronicles 20:3). His faith causes people from all over Judah to come together to seek help from God (v4). He prays in front of everyone, praising God (vv5-9). Even as he asks for help, he admits that he and his people are powerless to do anything: "We do not know what to do, but our eyes are upon you" (v12). Even the wives and children joined in this prayer.

We see God's answer, given by Jahaziel, one of the Levites (vv14-19). He told Jehoshaphat not to be discouraged or afraid, "For the battle is not yours, but God's" (v15). He

---

[4]Richard J. Foster, *Prayer: Finding the Heart's True Home* (London: Hodder & Stoughton, 1992), 89-90.

explained, "You will not have to fight this battle. Take up your positions; stand firm and see the deliverance the Lord will give you, O Judah and Jerusalem" (v17). After this incredible promise, Jehoshaphat falls down and worships God (v18). Then some Levites stand up and praise God with very loud voices (v19).

The next day, they set out for battle. Jehoshaphat encourages his people to have faith in God (v20). Verse 21 says,

After consulting the people, Jehoshaphat appointed men to sing to the Lord and to praise him for the splendor of his holiness as they went out at the head of the army, saying:

"Give thanks to the Lord,
for his love endures forever."

Just as they begin to sing and praise, God sets ambushes against the enemy armies. In the confusion, the three allied armies turn on each other and destroy each other (vv22-23). The vast army soon becomes a field of dead bodies. It took Jehoshaphat's men three days to collect the plunder from them (v25). On the fourth day they assembled in the Valley of Beracah to praise the Lord (v26). Indeed, "Beracah" means "praise" in Hebrew! That valley stands forever as a testimony to how much God's heart is moved when we praise him.

Praise in India

I believe one of the turning points in the ministry in India came when we started to praise and thank God more. In New Delhi in the summer of 1991, we decided we had to do more to help the poor in India. Each of the family groups in the church started visiting slums from time to time and helping the people. In this way we became aware of a colony of lepers, and we started frequently visiting and helping them. It made us appreciate how blessed we were—we had all our fingers and toes, our noses and eyes, our health, our jobs, our friends. These people once had normal lives, but now they had nothing. Our prayer lives changed as we were exposed to the suffering of the poor.

By February 1992, the leaders of the British Commonwealth world sector of our churches were visiting India. My friend Douglas Arthur wanted to visit the leprosy colony he had heard so much about. Everyone came back weeping and much more thankful for what we each had.

Soon after that, Kip McKean shared in a sermon how he had written down one thousand things to be grateful for, and he had prayed through his list. I decided to do that, and it made me feel extremely grateful to God. It is no coincidence that prayer, joy and gratitude are tied closely together in 1 Thessalonians 5:16-18: "Be joyful always; pray continually; give thanks in all circumstances, for this is God's will for you in Christ Jesus."

I believe our greater gratitude in India produced greater fruit to the glory of God. From July of 1991 to May of 1996, the Indian churches grew from four congregations with 489 members in one nation, to eighteen congregations with 2759 members in five nations. God blessed us to grow sixfold in less than five years, and we praised him and thanked him every step of the way!

Praise in Bangladesh

By March 1996, my wife and I were preparing to leave India. God had raised up Indian nationals for the work there, and it was time for us to step aside so they could lead (John 3:30). But we still had not planted a church in the nation of Bangladesh, with over 120 million lost souls. We knew of no Bangladeshi disciples anywhere in the world who were willing to go. So, we drafted a mission team of about five members to start the church, including Moses and Mamta Singh, and Prakash and Joyce D'Sa. (My wife joined us later, after Prakash and Joyce left.) On Saturday, March 9, just two days before we were due to land, the political opposition in Bangladesh called a nationwide, indefinite, total strike. Their goal was to topple the government, and all businesses were closed. Transport (other than ambulances and taxis) was not allowed to run. We were tempted not to go, but we prayed and went anyway.

When we landed, our local Bangladeshi contacts asked, "Why didn't you call—we would have told you not to come!" But we prayed, thanking God that he was in control of everything. We lost our meeting hall due to the violence associated with the strike, but we determined to devote ourselves to praising God. Every day our small group rose at 5:00 AM for our own personal devotional times of prayer and Bible study with the Lord. At 6:30 AM, all of us gathered for one hour of group prayer, in which we always praised and thanked God with great joy. From 7:30-8:15 AM we studied the Bible together and talked about God's plans for our city and country. Then we read the local newspaper, which described the violence of the previous day. Every day the strike worsened. There were more incidents of violence, more people getting killed, more people getting angry. As we went out to preach the Word each day, whenever God did a small miracle, we immediately praised and thanked him out loud. Though the nationwide strike was intense, we knew God would protect us.

The time came for my wife and children to join me. The day they were flying in, we read the morning paper. The strike activists had started attacking *all* vehicles on the roads, including airport vans, and even ambulances, the previous evening. A crowd had surrounded a van coming from the airport the day before. A Molotov cocktail was thrown into the van, destroying it and burning its occupants to death. Nadine and my three children—Hannah, Luke and Esther— were coming in just a few hours, and it was too late to stop them. We prayed and rented a van from the airport.

On the way home from the airport, we sang and praised God in the van. That day there was a huge demonstration in the center of town. We tried to avoid it, but suddenly, we could see the street filling with thousands of people ahead of us, running toward us. They were angry, and they surrounded our van. We had been singing and praising God all the way from the airport, but now we started begging him for help.

The people were screaming at us, beating on the van. My wife and children were inside. The driver was panicking. Our local friend was very afraid, too. We could not get out. More and more people surrounded us. Out of nowhere a man came and said, "Leave them alone." Then he disappeared into the crowd. Who was he? I do not know, but I am sure that God sent him to us. His words gave us the time to run out of the van. We carried our children and hid for more than an hour, waiting for the crowd to disperse. Then we walked and cycled with our luggage to where we would stay. And we praised God. We remembered the words of 2 Chronicles 20:17:

> "'You will not have to fight this battle. Take up your positions; stand firm and see the deliverance the Lord will give you, O Judah and Jerusalem. Do not be afraid; do not be discouraged. Go out to face them tomorrow, and the Lord will be with you.'"

Once my wife and children were in Bangladesh, we figured we had to make the most of it until we could safely get them out. Every day Nadine and I went out to study the Bible with people. Everyone had a lot of time to meet with us because no one could go to work or to the university—everything was on strike! God had arranged it so that our time would be very fruitful. We traveled by walking or by taking "cycle-rickshaws."

One night the cycle-rickshaw driver refused to take us all the way to our cheap hotel. He let us off about one hundred yards away. In the distance we could see a huge crowd of people surrounding the traffic circle near our hotel. We started to walk, when suddenly we heard a loud bang. Thousands of people were running down the road, straight at us! The police were chasing them and shooting into the crowd—we could hear the shots. The crowd was throwing bombs back at the police. Our children were right there, in the hotel, in a room by the window of the second floor, while this battle raged in the street below them. We were swept away by the crowd, running down the alleyways of this desperate city. Nadine and I burst into a small compound and ran right into a family's tin hut.

The man who owned the house was named Safi Uzzaman. Another man named Mr. Shahjahan was with us. There in the tin hut, Safi Uzzaman offered us tea and biscuits. Outside, in the alleyway, we could hear shotgun blasts just a few feet away from the thin tin walls of the hut. I had been very afraid when we faced danger in Bangalore six years earlier. But there, drinking tea in the middle of a civil war, I felt totally at peace. I knew God would protect us and our children. I could feel his presence, and I felt very happy that I was not afraid anymore.

After about an hour, the crowd had dispersed. We walked to our hotel. We could see the smoldering remains of bombs that had been thrown. We ran up to our room and discovered that our children were fine. Wendy D'Souza, who had been taking care of them, had turned off the lights and kept them away from the windows. She pretended that it was all a game. Nadine and I praised and thanked God from the bottom of our hearts that night—it was easy to do! He had done so much for us.

A few days later, we managed to get Nadine and the children out safely. I stayed to finish the work. Years later, in spite of many troubles, we now have twenty-two strong disciples in Bangladesh. For my family, it is truly our Valley of Praise.

I believe God was willing to help and protect us because we were willing to praise and thank him when we *were not* facing a crisis—it just was the way we lived. This is also how Jehoshaphat lived, long before the armies attacked him. God loves it when his people praise him from the heart. It is very easy to praise the things of this world: cars, houses, buildings, computers, electronic gadgets. But we have a relationship with the God who made infinitely more than all those things!

Practical Praise

I try to devote part of my prayer time every day to praise and thanksgiving. It is very encouraging to pray in this way! Let me give you a practical suggestion: have a different theme of praise and thanksgiving every day. Here are thirty ideas. (I am sure you can come up with more on your own.)

- The word of God—how awesome it is
- God's plan throughout history, from Adam to Abraham to David to Jesus (and everyone in between!)
- Creation
- The life of Jesus
- The Holy Spirit
- The cross

- The qualities of God
- The resurrection
- The miracles of Jesus
- God's blessings—spiritual (the blessings of being a Christian)
- God's blessings—in your personal life
- God's love
- God's power
- Heaven
- Technology—how God has allowed man to make machines that make life and evangelism easier
- Modern history
- Great men of God in church history
- Modern-day great men of God
- Your personal conversion story—all the steps that led you to God
- Each year of your life
- World evangelism—by city/country
- God's word, using Psalm 119
- The early church
- Answered prayers
- The Bible, book by book
- Failures and defeats in the Bible that God turned into victories
- The way God has taken care of your physical and financial needs all of your life
- A book of the Bible, verse by verse (read a verse, pray, read another verse, pray, etc.)
- Every member of your church
- Every friend you have ever had

Be the One

When Jesus healed the ten lepers, only one came back to give praise to God. Jesus was disappointed and he asked,

"Where are the other nine?" (Luke 17:17). May he never say the same of us. Let us give him praise and thanksgiving from the depths of our hearts! Let us find our own personal Valley of Praise and live there forever!

TAKING INVENTORY

1. *How is your praise life? Are your prayers just a series of requests, with an occasional thanksgiving for blessings? It is time to change, now, before you face a crisis.*

2. *Do you have a favorite psalm of praise? Which one? If not, find one and memorize it.*

3. *Write your own psalm of praise and thanksgiving, relating to some recent circumstances in your life. Pray through it, and then share it with a friend or two.*

15

Aggressive Prayer

So Jacob was left alone, and a man wrestled with him till daybreak. When the man saw that he could not overpower him, he touched the socket of Jacob's hip so that his hip was wrenched as he wrestled with the man. Then the man said, "Let me go, for it is daybreak."

But Jacob replied, "I will not let you go unless you bless me."

The man asked him, "What is your name?"

"Jacob," he answered.

Then the man said, "Your name will no longer be Jacob, but Israel, because you have struggled with God and with men and have overcome."

Genesis 32:24-28

More than any other passage of Scripture, this section on Jacob has influenced my prayer life. He was a sinful, self-dependent man. God kept sending him problems to teach him a lesson. Finally, all alone, Jacob wrestled with an angel of God all night long. The angel damaged Jacob, wrenching his hip, but even then, Jacob would not let him go. He said, "I will not let you go unless you bless me." And God blessed him!

Jacob was aggressive. He did not quit. He persevered. Sometimes God does not answer our prayers immediately because he *wants* us to persevere. We need to remember that the value of a great relationship with God is greater than the value of the things we are asking him for!

Jacob was called "Israel," which means "he struggles with God" (v28). He struggled with God and with men, and he overcame. In this passage at least, prayer is a contact sport. Similarly, in the New Testament, Epaphras was commended by Paul to the Colossians because he was "always wrestling in prayer for you" (Colossians 4:12).

Audacious Requests

Aggressive prayer is bold prayer. It asks for things that almost seem audacious. In Genesis 18, Abraham bargained with God over sinful Sodom. He questioned God's justice because God was willing to destroy the righteous with the unrighteous (Genesis 18:23). Abraham knew that he was being aggressive—in Genesis 18:27, he said, "Now that I have been so bold as to speak to the Lord, though I am nothing but dust and ashes...." He apologized again for his boldness (v30) and asked God not to be angry! (vv30, 32). This was bold, aggressive prayer, and it did not make God mad. Instead, God called Abraham his friend. God listened to his prayer and spared Abraham's nephew Lot and Lot's daughters.

Hundreds of years later, Esther faced the destruction of her people, the Jews. But God had placed her near to the king of Persia. She fasted for three days (Esther 4:15-16) and surely prayed for deliverance. This was aggressive prayer. God liked it, and he performed many miracles to save Esther, to save Mordecai (her adoptive father), and to save her people from the evil Haman.

Similarly, in Exodus 32, after the people made a golden calf, God was ready to destroy them (vv9-10). But Moses argued with God about his people's fate (vv11-13). God listened to Moses, relenting from bringing disaster on the people (v14). As the psalmist said, Moses "stood in the breach" to prevent God from destroying his people (Psalm 106:19-23).

Throughout history, God has looked for men and women who would have this type of relationship with him. In Ezekiel 22:30, he lamented,

"I looked for a man among them who would build up the wall and stand before me in the gap on behalf of the land so I would not have to destroy it, but I found none."

God longs for people to pray aggressively, to stand between heaven and hell, interceding for a lost and dying world. Will you be such a man? Will you be such a woman?

Aggressive prayer may sometimes seem presumptuous. Jesus said in Mark 11:23 that we should speak authoritatively *to the mountain*. Joshua told *the sun* to stand still in Joshua 10. Jesus commanded the wind and waves to stop (Mark 4:39). He commanded the deaf man's ears to open (Mark 7:34). He asked dead Lazarus to come out of the tomb (John 11:43). In Luke 5:13 he told the leper to "be clean." In Mark 1:25 he rebuked the evil spirit, telling it to come out of the man. These were bold, aggressive prayers, and God wanted them to be prayed.

Persevering Prayer

Aggressive prayer is also persevering prayer. It is the spirit of Jacob that should be in us when we pray, "I will not let you go unless you bless me!" Perseverance in prayer is also the point of Jesus' parables in Luke 11 and Luke 18. In

Luke 11:5-8, the master is locked inside his house, comfortable with his children, when a man knocks at his door at midnight, seeking help for a friend. Even though he will not answer because he is the man's friend, he will answer because of the man's boldness! That word can also be translated "persistence." In Luke 18:1-8, we see an unjust judge. He eventually answers the widow's request because she keeps bugging him. We must understand that God is *not* unjust, but he is moved by persistence.

Aggressive prayer keeps on trying, even when the answer has been no for a while. Once again, God wants us to understand that the value of a great relationship with him is greater than the value of what we ask him to do for us. Andrew Murray observed, "When our prayers are not answered, we learn that the fellowship and love of God are more to us than the answers of our requests, and then we continue in prayer."[1]

God wants us to wear him out with our prayers. Isaiah 62:6b-7 says,

> *You who call on the Lord,*
> *give yourselves no rest,*
> *and give him no rest till he establishes Jerusalem*
> *and makes her the praise of the earth.*

He is challenging us to keep bothering him till he answers. God loves it when we are aggressive in prayer! Many times we may give up in our prayers just before God was about to give the answer to us. We can be aggressive in our relationships with people, sometimes even being rude to get what we want, but when it comes to God, we can be as timid as mice. Actually, God wants us to be gentle with other people (Ephesians 4:1-2) and aggressive with him. We need to make

---

[1] Douglas Ed Cox and Edward A. Elliot, Sr., eds. *The Best of Andrew Murray on Prayer*, (Uhrichsville, Ohio: Barbour Publishing, Inc.), 18.

decisions to be aggressive in our prayers. We need to ask confidently and boldly because Jesus allows us to enter the Most Holy Place with confidence (Hebrews 10:19). We need to ask until he answers.

Praying for a Miracle

Sam and Emily Kanu are disciples in the church in London, and on November 30, 1996, their ten-year-old son, Joseph, began to complain of a headache. During the next few days it grew worse, making him vomit. On December 4, his parents rushed him to the accident and emergency section of the hospital. They prescribed paracetamol to Joseph and sent him home. Within a few hours he collapsed. This time he was admitted into the hospital and was diagnosed with meningitis. Sam and Emily started to pray.

An X-ray and MRI scan on December 7 confirmed the fears of the doctors. Joseph had streptococcal meningitis and the scans showed subdural empyema—a collection of pus around the brain. If the infection continued, the pressure on Joseph's brain would kill him. All over London, disciples prayed that God would save little Joseph.

The surgeons asked Sam and Emily to sign a consent form for a right frontal craniotomy. They were going to remove the front of Joseph's skull. The procedure would give Joseph a fifty-fifty chance of survival. They signed the necessary forms, and just after midnight on December 8, the five-hour operation began. Pus from around Joseph's brain was drained. Joseph went into a deep coma, kept alive by a ventilator.

During the following eight days, three further operations for drainage were carried out in a desperate attempt to control the infection. Even more desperate prayers, with fasting, were offered up to God by sincere disciples all over the UK. But on December 16, the surgeons told Sam and

Emily that their son would be dead within two days. "I remember what I told the surgeon," said Sam. "I told him: 'Listen, we believe in the power of God. As long as there is one iota of life in our son's body, God can work.'"

Sam and Emily had been praying desperately, finding comfort by studying Job and Psalms and by holding on to the promises of God. Psalm 37:4 was a focal promise of their prayers, but with this news, they began to pray with even more desperation. "We prayed with tears. We were intensely focused on God. There was no doubt in our minds that God was going to do what we asked of him: 'Give us back our son!'" remembers Sam. "We had been fasting by often missing meals, but now we began to fast more earnestly. For the next week we ate only in the evening to keep up our strength." They also knew that the whole London church was begging God to heal Joseph, and whenever brothers and sisters visited Joseph, they took time to pray together.

The children to the left and right of Joseph in the intensive care ward both died. "Were we going to be the next parents to lose their child?" thought Sam and Emily. Two more drainage operations followed. Then the surgeons said that even if Joseph survived, he would be severely brain damaged. They were making plans to move him to a hospital for severely disabled children.

However, God had been preparing a miracle. After three weeks of deep coma, when Joseph began to open his eyes and react to voices around him, his body was completely paralyzed. The doctors had no hope that he would walk again, but to the amazement of all who had cared for him, Joseph made a spectacular recovery! He sustained no permanent brain damage, and he can walk and run and play like any other child. He is now a strong thirteen-year-old, and his health continues to improve.

Sam says, "Whenever I see the surgeon, he always smiles and says, 'God is amazing, eh?' I want God to get all the glory." Sam and Emily never gave up as they prayed for their son. They were bold and persistent—and so was the whole London church. God hears aggressive prayer.

Praying for Fruit

Toye Oshunbiyi prayed consistently to baptize someone on the Sunday of the Men's Forum of the London church in April of 1999. The people he had been teaching the Bible to had one by one turned away from following Jesus. Faced with the prospect of not being evangelistically fruitful, Toye prayed desperately and remembered someone called Robert he had studied the Bible with eighteen months before. He rang him, and Robert's wife answered the phone. She told Toye that Robert had been in the hospital for several months.

On that Friday (the same day), Toye visited Robert in the hospital. Robert was virtually a paraplegic. He had had two operations on his neck and spine following a near-fatal car accident. The doctors were not sure whether he would walk again. He broke down and cried with joy on seeing Toye and begged him to teach him how to be a Christian. They studied intensely for three days. Robert still remembered everything that Toye had taught him before. On the third day, Robert was lifted into the baptistry on the Sunday evening of the Men's Forum. Toye baptized his friend on that day, just as he had prayed, and Robert is now saved. In the following weeks, after continued prayer, his medical condition rapidly improved. Robert is now walking, driving and working. Toye's aggressive prayers changed Robert's eternal destiny.

Praying Through Obstacles

Manju and Rani are two sisters from a very traditional family, living together in Pune, India. When they studied the

Bible and became Christians, family members were very upset. But these sisters are very strong in their convictions. They attended all the meetings of the church and went out sharing their faith with other disciples. Their father would come home drunk every night , so they started to pray that their father would leave his drinking habit. When their dad was sober, Manju and Rani shared with him scriptures they learned in church. Their mother saw that their faith was real, and she started becoming sympathetic to it.

After two years of regularly sharing the Bible with their dad, they saw him start to change. He stopped drinking and even started coming to church. Still, their attitude toward God was, "We won't let you go unless you bless us." A few months later their parents, Mahadu and Vasanthi, studied the Bible and became Christians! Now their parents get up every day at 4:00 AM to pray, and they are eternally grateful to their daughters for persevering in prayer!

Praying in the Final Hours

Several years ago we led the church in Kansas City. David Petty was dying of cancer in Wichita, Kansas. His wife, Laura, was a young disciple with two young children. The church in Wichita had not even started yet—there was only a faithful group of seventeen disciples. Many had prayed for David, but his heart was proud. However, as the cancer devoured his body, his heart grew softer. We fasted and prayed more, and he agreed to study the Bible.

Years of addictive sin had hardened his heart, yet Laura never gave up praying for him. Laura's and the Wichita church's aggressive prayers moved the heart of God. David Petty was baptized into Jesus, and just a few weeks later he went to be with God.

Now, nine years later, Laura is a strong disciple in the Wichita church. She is happily remarried to Jeff Hattendorf.

Jenna and Shelby, Laura's children, are extremely happy because God has given them a new stepdad who loves them very much.

Praying for Years

In December 1986, the Bangalore mission team landed in India for a two-month language internship. We were a loony, inexperienced bunch, with much faith and creativity. On December 28, Douglas Cruz and I were evangelizing together, and we invited a young man named John Emmanuel. He immediately responded very positively. We studied the Bible together and about three weeks later he was baptized into Christ—one of the first converts in God's movement in India!

At the start of February 1987, the mission team had to return to London for more training, so we left John and three other converts behind, promising we would be back. Eleven months later, we returned to plant the church, and John was still faithful. We started a Bible discussion in his home in East Bangalore that bore much fruit. Sadly, after about six months, John got discouraged and left the Lord. We were all heartbroken. He was such a gentle and kind man, and he had been very helpful to us.

Though John left God, God never forgot him—and neither did we. I frequently mentioned him in my prayers and wrote cards to him through the years. On September 30, 1993, John was in Solapur, Maharashtra, in the middle of an earthquake (7.6 on the Richter scale). Ten thousand people died, and tens of thousands were left homeless. But John's village was spared, even though villages all around were flattened. This made him really think about God. John said, "That night I walked out of my house, and the dust was floating in the air like the fallout from an atom bomb. The ground was shaking." Yet, he still did not return to God. He got married, had children and moved on with his life, but we could never forget him.

Finally, in the summer of 1999, six years after the earthquake, John started working with a young man named Daniel in Bombay. This man was not open to Christianity, but he had been to the church and had studied the Bible with the brothers. He did not want to change his life, so he brought John Emmanuel to the brothers to prove to them that "not everyone from your church is committed." However, when John met the brothers, he knew it was time to change, much to Daniel's amazement. He studied the Bible, was restored, and his wife is now visiting the church. He is extremely happy.

During all those years in which God was seemingly "doing nothing" in response to our prayers and letters to John, the Holy Spirit was working in his life. Eleven years of aggressive prayer were well worth it in the end! The East Region of the Bangalore church, which started with one disciple twelve years ago—John—now has more than 250 members!

Wrestling in Prayer

There is an angel waiting to wrestle you. There is a hungry man outside, needing bread. There is a widow who needs justice. There are cities about to be destroyed. It is time to be aggressive in our prayers, instead of being aggressive in our relationships. As James said, "You quarrel and fight. You do not have, because you do not ask God" (James 4:2). We all need to pray the prayer of Jacob: "I will not let you go unless you bless me."

TAKING INVENTORY

1. How do you feel about aggressive prayers? What does your answer reveal about your character?

2. What was the most aggressive prayer you have ever prayed since you have been a disciple? Has it been answered yet?

3. What have you stopped praying about? Why? How will you change?

16

Creative Prayer

This is what the Lord says:

"Cursed is the one who trusts in man,
who depends on flesh for his strength
and whose heart turns away from the Lord.
He will be like a bush in the wastelands;
he will not see prosperity when it comes.
He will dwell in the parched places of the desert,
in a salt land where no one lives.

"But blessed is the man who trusts in the Lord,
whose confidence is in him.
He will be like a tree planted by the water
that sends out its roots by the stream.
It does not fear when heat comes;
its leaves are always green.
It has no worries in a year of drought
and never fails to bear fruit."

Jeremiah 17:5-8

Jeremiah described two kinds of spiritual life in this passage. One man's life is dry and empty, depending on human flesh for strength. The other man's life is like a "tree planted by streams of water." He is the "Psalm-One Man," fruitful and prosperous (Psalm 1:3).

Keeping It Fresh

Creativity makes all the difference in our relationship with God. We must always remain open to ways of keeping our relationship with God fresh, or our prayers will become one more example of human effort in our lives. How can we keep our relationship with God fresh? If you are looking for a formula, you will not find one here. The very nature of creativity is that a list or a set of rules cannot define it. It comes from the heart. It comes when we make an effort. Creativity comes when we are still in love with God. Jesus rebuked the church in Ephesus in Revelation 2:2-5:

> *I know your deeds, your hard work and your persever-ance. I know that you cannot tolerate wicked men, that you have tested those who claim to be apostles but are not, and have found them false. You have persevered and have en-dured hardships for my name, and have not grown weary.*
> *Yet I hold this against you: You have forsaken your first love. Remember the height from which you have fallen! Repent and do the things you did at first. If you do not re-pent, I will come to you and remove your lampstand from its place.*

The Ephesians were working hard. They were persevering. They were intolerant of sin. They had endured hardships. They were not tired of following Jesus. But they were not in love with God anymore. They had lost the love they had at first, so Jesus told them to do the things they did at first. Do what you used to do as a young Christian. Go crazy for God! Do not get stuck in a rut.

For example, I remember Ron Drabot sharing how he had "dates" with God or "cornflakes with the Lord." He really inspired me. Just like a romantic relationship needs that special touch to keep the spark of love alive, so our walk with God needs creativity.

Since he is not a legalistic God, looking for formulas, one simple thing you can do is vary your posture in prayer. You can try different positions: kneel, raise your hands, dance, run, squat, swim, walk outdoors, eat and drink with God. Consider some examples from the Bible:

- Moses prayed with hands raised in Exodus 17:11-12. (See also Exodus 9:29.)
- Elisha prayed while lying on the dead boy in 2 Kings 4:33-34.
- David danced before the Lord in 2 Samuel 6:14.
- John fell prostrate in Revelation 1:17.
- Jesus walked on the water while praying in Matthew 14:23-25.
- Daniel got down on his knees to pray in Daniel 6:10.

The heart of God definitely is moved by creative prayer. In 2 Kings 19, Hezekiah was faced with the powerful armies of Assyria. They had destroyed everything in their path. They wrote a threatening letter to him, letting him know that Jerusalem was to be their last conquest. So, he tore his clothes and went into the temple of the Lord (v1). He spread the letter out before God and prayed about it (vv14-19). He praised God. He begged God. His prayer was from the heart; it was not a ritual. And God saved Israel, sending an angel who destroyed 185,000 Assyrian troops in one night! (2 Kings 19:35-37).

Keeping in Step

I remember when Mark Pichamuthu, one of the evangelists in New Delhi, went out with me to share the gospel with lost souls one morning in April of 1993. We prayed that God would lead us to open souls that very day. We were determined to be fresh in our walk with God, not legalistic. We shared our faith in a business complex, praying and going up and down the halls of the complex. I decided to go wherever I felt the Holy Spirit was leading me. At one point I felt drawn down a narrow hallway, where four young men were speaking to each other. I prayed and spoke to them. One of them was interested in talking to me. His name was Raj Kumar, and he gave me his address. That same day he came to a group Bible discussion at my house. Just two weeks later he was baptized. Now, six years later, he is happily married and a leader in the New Delhi church.

Later that morning we were still praying for fruit. I saw a friendly man walking across a plaza in the business complex. I spoke with him and he gave me his number. I had a conviction that he was open. That week I went out of town, and he came to church that Sunday. But he never came again after that, and I gave up on him. About nine months later I was praying, and I was reminded of that friendly young man, Sushil Panna. I called him up at work. He was very glad to talk to me. He came to church and was baptized in January, 1994. He, too, is now happily married and a leader in the New Delhi church. Our morning of prayer and evangelism led us to two wonderful souls who are now powerful leaders in the kingdom of God! When our hearts strive to be creative as we walk with God, he blesses our efforts more than we can ask or imagine!

The Bangladeshi List

As I wrote previously, we went to Bangladesh during a civil war to start a church there in 1996. Before we went, we thought of Hezekiah. The challenge before us was immense: we had no mission team, no one who could speak the language, and the nation was in political and economic turmoil. On a small sheet of paper we wrote the numbers one through eleven. Number one was a place to meet. We found out the day we landed that the place we had booked earlier was unavailable, so we had no meeting hall. The one item on our list that we had already filled in was cancelled! Number two was a place to live for the mission team. In a Muslim nation, hotels are associated with sinful behavior, and it was essential to rapidly get a ministry base in a home. However, this was no easy task with a nationwide strike, as no real estate agents were working.

Number three was to find a place to baptize people. This can be a very challenging task in a Muslim nation where conversion is illegal and large plastic water tanks are not available. Numbers four to eleven were blank. They were the names of our mission team! We asked God that we might meet eight people by March 31, 1996 (in twenty-one days), who by that date would be baptized, or on their way to being baptized.

Every day, during our morning devotionals, we spread out our list before God, just like Hezekiah. We asked him to fill it. We carried a copy with us. One by one, we saw God answer our prayers. On that Tuesday, the day after we landed, we asked God to give us a hall to meet in by noon. We separated and went out. When we met together again at twelve, one of the team members, Moses, announced that he had found a meeting hall. Three days later we had our first church service. The five of us had fifty-one people at church, in the middle of a civil war, with no cars or buses running and everyone on strike. God answered our prayers!

Within two weeks we found an excellent flat for Moses and Mamta to live in, one which we used safely for more than three years.

Item number three, the baptistry, was hard to find. We went to an industrial supplies yard, and there we found an old drum used to store chemicals. They sold it to us and washed it out, and we had a baptistry.

Our most important prayers were to find open souls. Our mission team had no Bangladeshi members. We were desperate to find local people who could help us. While praying a few years earlier, I had stopped and invited a young man to church in New Delhi. He turned out to be a Bangladeshi of Christian origin who was in town so that his wife could have an operation in Delhi. Edward came to church in Delhi, and we wrote to each other regularly.

When we landed in Bangladesh, Edward was ready to help us. By the end of the three weeks, he and his wife had been baptized, as well as his nephew and another young man. Besides those four, there were another *five* people who were studying the Bible at the end of March who were baptized in the following months. God gave us everything on our list! I believe he was moved by our creative prayers and also by our creative efforts to see those prayers come true.

Raising Holy Hands

One of the evangelists in Bangalore really inspired me by his creative prayer life. Saji Joseph was one of the first men baptized by Dinesh George in the Cochin, Kerala, church in 1992. He later married a fine young lady named Sonia and went on staff in Bangalore. In March 1999, Saji had it on his heart to draw close to God. He was inspired by another leader's message about the power of prayer. In this message, the brother made a point about how Moses prayed in Exodus 17:9-14 while raising his hands, and God brought victory to the Israelites. Saji wanted to imitate Moses, so he decided to pray for twenty-four hours straight, with his hands raised.

Saji knew that this would be very challenging. He later shared, "I was a bit afraid about the task because I knew the pain I would have to go through. I started thinking scientifically that the blood in my hands would stop, my shoulder joints would become weak, etc. But I took courage from Moses' example and decided to do it." Saji prepared a schedule for the prayer, including what to pray for and whom to pray with. He started his prayer on March 19, 1999, at 11:00 PM. Brothers from his ministry came in forty-five minute shifts to hold up his arms.

Saji was very creative in his prayer. He praised God, thanked God, confessed his sins, prayed through the Psalms, sang spiritual songs to God and prayed for all the disciples in the church. He prayed for all the South Asian churches and leaders, for all the work for the poor, for all the churches in the world (one by one) and for all his family. He also prayed for all of the workers on staff in the South Asian churches, for the leaders of the churches around the world, for many specific miracles and for much fruit. Saji said later,

> I am thankful to the disciples who held my hands up. After three hours, my hands turned cold and numb. After seven hours, I started feeling that my hands were cut off. Many young and weak Christians came forward to help in prayer and hold my hands up. Both they and I were very much inspired.
>
> By the end of twenty-four hours, I was definitely tired physically, but I was charged spiritually. For almost a week, I could not lift my arms or move my shoulders. I finished my prayer on March 20 at 12:00 PM. A few days

later, I decided to pray for another twenty-four hours, this time without raising my hands.

The following month, God blessed Saji's region of the church (250 members) with eighteen new souls added.

Keeping Watch

Saji's wife, Sonia, was equally creative and radical. She had been a disciple for several years and had seen seven women whom she had personally invited become Christians. However, each of these seven had left the Lord, and this very much disappointed her. So she decided in September 1999 to fast from sleep for one hundred hours, using each night to pray alone, all night long. She was desperate for "fruit that will last" (John 15:16) and creative in the way she cried out to God. Each day Sonia was active in the ministry, focused on God. Each night she prayed all night. By sixty hours she was very sleepy, and actually fell asleep for fifteen minutes. But she woke up and continued her fast. She read the Psalms, walked around and did everything to continue to stay awake. She continued like this for ninety hours, just short of her goal, when she accidentally fell asleep for the night.

God was moved by Sonia's faith. A few weeks later, as she was on her way to encourage Alphonsamma, a disciple who was bedridden, she met a wonderful young lady named Tara. Tara studied the Bible and made her decision for Christ in October, and Sonia is confident that she will never leave the Lord! Our creative prayers move the heart of God.

Two or More

"Again, I tell you that if two of you on earth agree about anything you ask for, it will be done for you by my Father in

heaven. For where two or three come together in my name, there am I with them." (Matthew 18:19-20)

When I pray together with Nadine, which is a daily habit, it bonds us close together. When the mission team went to Bangladesh and all of us prayed together for an hour a day, we were ready for anything. I often pray together with the brothers I disciple to Christ. What better way can there be for two disciples to pass the time when they are together? When you pray with someone, it bonds you together. Small attitudes and reservations melt away, and your creativity is stimulated.

Are you a bush, or are you a tree planted by a stream? The Scriptures, this book and the examples we have shared will hopefully inspire you to fall in love with God again, to be creative and to see your prayers come alive like never before. Why not start today?

TAKING INVENTORY

1. *What is your prayer life like? Is it like a bush in the wastelands or like a lush tree, planted by a stream? How can you tell?*

2. *If your prayer life has gone stale, let me make one suggestion: pray with a strong brother or sister for an hour. Remember that Jesus promised to be there whenever two or more are gathered (Matthew 18:19-20). If Jesus is there, you know the prayer time will be awesome!*

3. *Choose or find a creative prayer type and schedule it in soon.*

17

Tears

During the days of Jesus' life on earth, he offered up prayers and petitions with loud cries and tears to the one who could save him from death, and he was heard because of his reverent submission.

Hebrews 5:7

Jesus prayed with loud cries and tears. This was not just in the garden of Gethsemane (Luke 22:44), but "during the days of Jesus' life on earth." He wept over Jerusalem (Luke 19:41-44) just a few months before thousands would be baptized there on the day of Pentecost (Acts 2:41). His prayers were passionate, full of emotion and heart. And his Father listened.

The God who wipes the tears from our eyes answers the prayers of those who cry. He is rich in mercy and compassion and is moved by our tears. Even here on earth among sinners, there is something about a little child crying that moves the hardest of hearts.

Jesus Wept

In John 11, Jesus got the bad news that his friend Lazarus was sick in Bethany (v3). By the time he arrived there,

Lazarus had already been dead for four days (v17). When Mary reached Jesus, she told him the same words as her sister Martha: "Lord, if you had been here, my brother would not have died" (vv21, 32), but unlike Martha, Mary had been weeping. And Jesus was moved. John 11:33 says, "When Jesus saw her weeping, and the Jews who had come along with her also weeping, he was deeply moved in spirit and troubled." He immediately wanted to do something to help (v34). Their tears moved his heart. He himself wept (v35). He went to the tomb, and said a simple, faithful prayer, commanding Lazarus to come out (vv41-43). And the dead man walked out of the tomb (v44).

We must never underestimate the power of our tears when we pray. The difference between Martha and Mary in this passage is that Mary cried. Martha loved her brother, but it was Mary's tears (and her friends' tears) that moved the heart of Jesus and the heart of God. Similarly, Jesus was moved by the widow of Nain (Luke 7:11-19), and he saw how much Jairus loved his daughter (Mark 5:21-24, 36-43). He acted on their tears, raising their loved ones from the dead! Also, in the Old Testament, Hezekiah was told that he would die. But he prayed with tears , and God saw his tears and heard his prayer, adding fifteen years to his life (2 Kings 20:1-6).

God sees every tear we cry. And when we cry in prayer, it touches his heart. As it is written in Psalm 126:5-6,

> *Those who sow in tears*
> *will reap with songs of joy.*
> *He who goes out weeping,*
> *carrying seed to sow,*
> *will return with songs of joy,*
> *carrying sheaves with him.*

Parents' Tears

In the summer of 1992 we were in New Delhi leading the church, and Nadine was pregnant with our second child. She had already suffered one miscarriage in 1991, and she was in the seventh month of this pregnancy. One evening I went out with the staff to see a Hindi film, and I left Nadine at home so she could rest. When I came home, I found her on her back, crying. She had slipped and fallen while tidying up Hannah's room, and she could not get up. Significant amounts of water had come out of her uterus. I helped her up and called a taxi to take us to the hospital, knowing that care for premature babies in India was virtually nonexistent at that time. While we waited for a taxi, I got on my knees and said a simple prayer to God, weeping for the life of our son in Nadine's womb. I reaffirmed to God my commitment to give Luke to him for all his days. Nadine also passionately begged God to spare our child.

We reached the hospital and Nadine was put under observation for several days. Though we thought that her water had broken, somehow she was able to go to full term with the pregnancy. Luke was born happy and healthy on August 21, 1992. I am sure that God saw the tears of his desperate servants that day.

A Daughter's Tears

Samantha Devadas became a disciple in 1988. From the day of her baptism, she had it on her heart to win her parents to Jesus Christ. She prayed daily, often with loud cries and tears, for God to save her family. For many years there was no progress. But God had seen her tears. Seven and a half years later God answered her prayer, when her mother, Lizzie Devadas, was baptized. Within six months her father, John Devadas, became a Christian—and her grandmother, Sarah Luke, was also saved. God sees the tears of his people.

Tears of Desperation

Jolly grew up in Kerala, India. She had loved Jesus since her childhood, but she always knew there was something missing in her life. She thought that only saints in ancient legends could truly be godly. While doing her training as a nurse, she was exposed to the wickedness and cruelty of this world as she saw injured people in the hospital, often having been abused by their own families. She decided to make a difference by caring for just one person. Jolly began to take care of a lady who had endured a hard life with many struggles. But without God, the friendship turned to immorality.

Jolly knew that she had sinned, and she went to the Hindu temples in search of God. But the idols there did not inspire her. She prayed to Mary, but still there was something missing in her life. She became increasingly desperate in her search for God, even taking time off from work to go to church halls and pray. Finally, in complete desperation, she prayed and fasted for four days continuously, without food or water, crying out, "God, if you are there, then please show me the right way." She spoke to priests and read holy books, but still there was no answer, although she was praying ever more desperately. Then one day, on a table in the intensive care unit where she worked, Jolly found an invitation to the Delhi Church of Christ.

Jolly explained, "I realized that this invitation was the answer to my prayers. I went along with a friend to the place on the card. I saw people loving each other and taking care of each other. God can give us immeasurably more than what we ask or imagine."

He saw all her tears, and she became a Christian. Now, nine years later, Jolly is happily married to Saji Geevarghese. They have three children, and they run poverty projects serving children, prisoners and slum-dwellers in Bombay, India.

A Young Man's Tears

Fred Scott was baptized into Christ in November of 1984. He was a faithful, zealous young man, with a bright future in the kingdom of God. In the autumn of 1985, he felt a lump in his knee. When he went to the doctor, they discovered that Fred had advanced osteogenic sarcoma (bone cancer). In a matter of weeks, Fred's world was turned upside down. He endured a never-ending string of hospital visits and chemotherapy. He was X-rayed, poked and prodded, and faced with the prospect that he would die as a young man. He was hospitalized, and he lost his hair as he lay in a ward where people all around him were dying, one by one.

Most of us in the young London church visited him. Led by Douglas Arthur, many prayed with loud cries and tears for this special young man. But surely the one who prayed with the most passion was Fred. I'm going to let Fred tell the story in his own words:

I had been a Christian for about a year when a visit to the doctor yielded a surprising result—an X-ray of my left leg revealed a rather large, suspected bone tumor around the knee joint. I thought the concerned-looking registrar was joking when he hinted at the implications (surgery, amputation, etc.). I explained that as an aspiring Bible talk leader in my church, I didn't have time for such things and that this sort of thing didn't happen to a twenty-four-year-old!

I was told to report back to the hospital on Sunday night after that appointment, which was before the weekend. I obtained leave from the doctor to attend the London church's student retreat, as long as I showed up on Sunday for a Monday morning biopsy and other tests.

The weekend was characterized by many emotions, ranging from denial to fear. One evening at the retreat, Chris McGrath (my discipler and best friend, now leading the church in Detroit) and I stood before a lake and poured out our hearts to God with loud cries and tears about the situation. I did not want to enter into the future and its attendant medical challenges without God. Anyone (other than God) who heard us that night would have attested that the sadness, wrestling, resignation and final praise and thanksgiving could only be pouring out of deeply troubled and distressed people!

For me, the following days, weeks and months were a stern test of faith as it was discovered that I had osteogenic sarcoma, an aggressive and usually fatal form of bone cancer. Radical, mutilating surgery was followed by months of grueling chemotherapy.

It is essential to get over the "Why me?" stage early if you want to survive the treatments. I had no shortage of prayer partners willing to visit me and find a niche in the draughty hospital corridors and staircases to pray. Often there would be tears; if I were to die, as seemed the most likely outcome, I wanted God to use me to touch the hearts of my family and friends in whatever way necessary in order to reach them.

Doug Arthur asked me one night "Freddie, are you ready to die?" I can honestly say that the answer was yes. Desperation draws you to God and you end up wanting to be with him more than anything else. My prayer became simple: "God, if you are going to let me live, then let my life count for your kingdom. I will do anything you set before me to the limit of my ability, and I know you will make up the difference."

The weeks became months, but the prayers, with tears, never ceased. And God did a miracle in young Fred's life. To the doctors' great encouragement and amazement, the cancer went into remission. Fred began to heal. Fourteen years have passed and Fred is still grateful for every single day that

God gives him. The cancer has not returned. Fred is married to Emma, and they have two lovely children—Lily and Jack. He is a geographic sector leader for the United Kingdom churches and a powerful evangelist in the now much larger London church that once prayed for his life. He and his wife Emma are very special to me and Nadine, and to many, many others.

God chose to spare Fred's life. He could not ignore the many tears shed as brothers and sisters prayed for Fred. There are times when we weep, but God still does not answer our prayers in the way we would like. We must pray according to his will (1 John 5:14), and sometimes what God wants to do is not what we want him to do. Jesus himself could not save his own life as he wept in the garden of Gethsemane. We cannot always understand what God is doing in our lives. But I am certain of this: when we weep, it moves God's heart. It makes him eager to help us. It makes him ready to do miracles. It unlocks the power of heaven.

Passionate Prayers

The special son of one of Elisha's good friends died (2 Kings 4). When the boy's mother came to Elisha for help, the prophet's servant, Gehazi, ran ahead and obeyed Elisha's instructions, but there was no response from the boy (v31). He went through the motions, but there was no heart, no passion. However, when Elisha saw the boy, he was passionate. He prayed and stretched himself out on the boy, mouth to mouth, eyes to eyes, hands to hands (v34). And God raised this boy from the dead (v35). When we are passionate, like Elisha, it moves the heart of God.

What a tragedy when we see an urgent need, but we pray without passion. How sad that we cannot shed a tear when we live in a world full of pain. Our Lord went through this world weeping for those in pain around him. Paul said in

Romans 9:2, "I have great sorrow and unceasing anguish in my heart," because his people, the Jews, were lost.

God wants to answer you when you pray to him. But maybe he is waiting for a tear, for some sign of deep feeling. He wants you to cry out in passion, not mumble in a ritual. I have heard Kip McKean say, "Our baptistries should be filled with the tears of our members. Tears for lost souls." I say amen to that. Our tears move the heart of God. Let us pray with passion and watch him change our world!

TAKING INVENTORY

1. *When was the last time you cried for someone other than yourself in your prayers?*

2. *Perhaps you need to be more in touch with your emotions. Writing out how you are feeling about different areas of your life is a good way to get in touch.*

3. *Ask some of your friends about answers to tear-filled prayers. Think about your own. What do you learn about God's character from them?*

Epilogue

As I have written this book, I have been deeply convicted of my own inadequacy in my walk with God. I am very eager to take it higher, to grow and to change. That is my desire for you, as well. I want you to walk away from this book with a new, better picture of God. I want you to see him as Isaiah saw him, as Jesus saw him. I want you to experience a turning point in your walk with God, just as Enoch did when he turned sixty-five.

Our God is a God who runs through the fields for us. He crawls through the gutters for us. He spreads out his arms to embrace us. He carries us in his arms. He wipes away our tears when we cry. He treasures us like jewels. He sings to us. He is an awesome, holy God, like a consuming fire. He is more powerful than we can imagine. He is preparing a place for us in heaven. I want to know this God. I want *you* to know this God. I want my family and friends to know this God. I want everyone to know this God!

We are called to walk in the footsteps of Jesus. A relationship with God is not a selfish, inwardly-focused act, but the living expression of a righteous man who longs to change the world. Proverbs 15:29 tells us, "The Lord is far from the wicked, but he hears the prayer of the righteous." As James said, "The prayer of a righteous man *is* powerful and effective" (James 5:16, emphasis added). I believe this with all my heart. I pray that you will learn to pray with *impact*, using some of the ideas in the second part of this book:

I   Intimate Prayer
M   Mighty Prayer
P   Praise and Thanksgiving

A   Aggressive Prayer
C   Creative Prayer
T   Tears

I pray that the examples in this book will give you faith. I pray you will open your eyes and see the miracles all around you. I pray you can see your family (and mine!) come to Christ. I pray all your dreams will come true. Let us walk with God together and change our world in this generation!

Appendix

When God Says No

To keep me from becoming conceited because of these surpassingly great revelations, there was given me a thorn in my flesh, a messenger of Satan, to torment me. Three times I pleaded with the Lord to take it away from me. But he said to me, "My grace is sufficient for you, for my power is made perfect in weakness." Therefore I will boast all the more gladly about my weaknesses, so that Christ's power may rest on me. That is why, for Christ's sake, I delight in weaknesses, in insults, in hardships, in persecutions, in difficulties. For when I am weak, then I am strong.

2 Corinthians 12:7-10

At some of the hardest times in our lives, we cry out to the Lord. We plead. We persevere. We believe. We weep. We purge sin out of our lives. Yet still he does not answer. Like Paul, we beg for healing. But the answer comes back as "No" or "Wait." We stand at the funerals of loved ones, asking "Why?" We hurt as we see people turn away from God. Our dreams are swept away; marriages dissolve; doors are closed. Yet we have prayed with all our hearts. And we ask, "Where is the Lord?" Or we wonder if he really loves us.

In Good Company

When God does not answer our prayers, at least not in the way we expected, how should we feel? First of all, we should remember that we are in good company. Paul was not the only one in the Bible who pleaded with God, only to find his prayers unanswered. In Numbers 12:7-8, God calls Moses "faithful in all my house," yet just a few verses later, when Moses' sister, Miriam, is leprous, God refuses to heal her (Numbers 12:11-15). In Deuteronomy 3:23-28 Moses refers to another time God refused to grant his request. In 2 Samuel 12:16-18, David fasted and pleaded with God for the life of his sick child, but the child died. Both 2 Samuel 21:14 and 24:25 say that there was a time when again God "answered prayer in behalf of the land," implying that he had not been answering up to that point. The Psalmist wrote, "O Lord God Almighty, how long will your anger smolder against the prayers of your people?" (Psalm 80:4).

The prophets also cried out to God, only to see their prayers not always answered. In Jeremiah 14:11-12, the Scripture says,

> Then the Lord said to me, "Do not pray for the well-being of this people. Although they fast, I will not listen to their cry; though they offer burnt offerings and grain offerings, I will not accept them."

In Jeremiah 15:1, God said, "Even if Moses and Samuel were to stand before me, my heart would not go out to this people." Habakkuk said,

> How long, O Lord, must I call for help,
>   but you do not listen?
> Or cry out to you, "Violence!"
>   but you do not save?
> Why do you make me look at injustice?
>   Why do you tolerate wrong?" (Habakkuk 1:2-3)

In the New Testament, surely John the Baptist and his disciples prayed for John's deliverance, yet he was executed by Herod. Surely Jesus prayed for Judas to stay faithful, yet he left the Lord. Surely the brothers and sisters in Acts 12 prayed not only for Peter, but also for James; yet James was executed, while Peter was spared.

Of course, perhaps the most powerful example of what looks to us like unanswered prayer is that of the Lord himself in the garden of Gethsemane. There he was, deeply sorrowful and troubled. There he prayed earnestly through the night. His sweat was like drops of blood. An angel appeared and strengthened him (Luke 22:39-44), yet God did not take the cup of suffering away from him: he still had to die on the cross. Indeed, his "unanswered" prayer helped him to accept God's will for his life. As he left Gethsemane, he was ready to die. But on the cross, he quoted Psalm 22, where David said,

> *My God, my God, why have you forsaken me?*
> *Why are you so far from saving me,*
> *so far from the words of my groaning?*
> *O my God, I cry out by day, but you do not answer,*
> *by night, and am not silent. (Psalm 22:1-2)*

When I see that God did not answer yes to the prayers of Jesus and so many other great people of God, it comforts me when my prayers are not answered as I had hoped. At least I am in good company!

All of these people loved God. Some of them had sin in their lives. Some of them were praying for people with sin in their lives. Some of them, including Jesus, were asking for things that were not in the will of God (1 John 5:14 says that if we ask according to God's will, he hears us). But with many of these prayers, there is no clear explanation. Why did God say no?

Why Does God Say No?

We must understand that there are times when God does not answer our prayers because we cherish sin in our hearts. I am not talking about temptation—all of us are tempted. I am not talking about character weaknesses or sins like selfishness, pride, laziness and impatience that we may fall into and then regret. What I mean is that if we are repetitively involved in sinful behavior, failing to confess or change it, cherishing the sin in our hearts, then the Scriptures teach that God will not hear our prayers (Psalm 66:17-19). David's child in 2 Samuel 12, conceived through his adultery with Bathsheba, most likely was not healed because of the sin in David's life. Though David had repented, his sin still had consequences, and his innocent child perished.

Sometimes God does not answer our prayers because he knows better than we do what is best for the people for whom we are praying. Isaiah 57:1 is an amazing verse:

> The righteous perish,
>   and no one ponders it in his heart;
> devout men are taken away,
>   and no one understands
> that the righteous are taken away
>   to be spared from evil.

Sometimes God may allow our loved ones to die in order to spare them from evil or suffering; at other times he knows their deaths will somehow benefit many others, so he allows them to be taken away (like his own Son). As we stand at the gravesides of our loved ones asking why, we must remember this passage.

At other times God may see that the people or churches we are praying for are unrepentant and that only hardship will turn them to the truth. This is what Jeremiah experienced in Jeremiah 14-15. And there are times when God's justice will not allow him to grant a request, as when he rejected Moses' prayer for Miriam in Numbers 12.

One other factor that we must consider when God does not answer our requests is that perhaps we are "fair-weather" friends. If we only come to him in our time of need, but ignore him and depend on ourselves otherwise, he may allow even further hardships in order to teach us to depend on him. Surely Paul prayed at the beginning of his hardships in Asia. Yet the troubles became worse and worse, to the point that Paul and his companions "despaired even of life" (2 Corinthians 1:8). Yet Paul recognized that "this happened that we might not rely on ourselves but on God, who raises the dead" (2 Corinthians 1:9). If Paul had to learn this lesson, certainly we must learn it, too.

Sometimes our prayers are not according to the will of God (1 John 5:14). We may not know this right then, but he has a plan, infinitely greater than our own agenda. Paul tried to preach in Bithynia, but God would not let him in there to preach. God wanted him to go to Macedonia instead (Acts 16:6-10). Surely Paul had prayed about his plans—but God had other plans! Many times I have seen God block my own ministry plans and ideas in order to guide me to his plans.

Finally, I must add that we cannot expect God to obey our every command if we pray to him in just the right way. When we expect our prayers, done in just the right way, to automatically produce miracles, then we are trying to become God ourselves, manipulating the Lord to do our bidding. In our hearts we must always remember that we are the servants and he is the Lord. He can do whatever he pleases, and like Job, we must fall down and worship him. When Job questioned God, God responded by asking, "Would you discredit my justice? Would you condemn me to justify yourself?" (Job 40:8). We must be careful not to become angry with God when he does not do as we wish. We can talk to him about how we feel, but we must surrender ourselves, as Jesus did at Gethsemane, accepting his will for our lives.

Personal Pain

Like all disciples, I have experienced the heartache of unanswered prayers. Indeed, I have experienced it many, many times. We prayed for Fred Scott to be healed of cancer in 1985. He was healed. Yet I also prayed for Khee Tay, another brother with cancer. I and many others visited him countless times, fasting and begging God for his deliverance. But he died of cancer that same year. My Uncle Augusto died of cancer a few years ago in Italy, in spite of many prayers. My Italian grandmother died just a few months ago, without ever responding to the gospel. I had prayed for her for fifteen years. She deteriorated so quickly that my prayer to be there when she died was not granted either. Each of these unanswered prayers was very painful to endure, and there was no obvious reason (to me) why God did not respond. Yet I love my Father in heaven, and I know he loves me, even when he does not answer the way I would like.

I have prayed for fruit when sharing my faith many times, and yet often did not see the fruit come. I have prayed for people to stay faithful, and yet they have walked away from God. I have prayed for people to become Christians, and yet they have rejected the gospel. I have prayed for the church to achieve great goals, and yet we have often fallen short. I have fasted; I have wept; I have fallen on the ground; I have persevered. And yet I have received the answer "No" or "Wait" again and again. Indeed, if I were to share about all my unanswered prayers, one by one, this book could be considerably longer. I am sure many of you have experienced the same thing.

I remember in 1994, I was leading the Delhi church. I prayed and begged God for the church to grow. I fasted. I wept. But no matter how much I prayed, people kept leaving the Lord, and many turned away from being baptized. On my knees I wept and asked God to change things. Finally, in 1995 the church experienced a great revival. From my limited perspective, many souls were lost as God said no. But only God's perspective is perfect and all-encompassing; only he understands what is needed for the evangelization of India and the world.

The miracle stories of our work in Bangladesh (shared in chapters 14 and 16) were real and were very encouraging. Yet in 1999, some dear friends of mine in that church became divisive, and we had to ask them to leave the fellowship. This was in spite of much prayer and fasting, and many tears. It broke our hearts. It deeply hurt the church. To this day, they are still lost. Was God saying no to me? His longing to see this couple restored is surely greater than that of anyone in the church. But in his mercy, he allows people to have free will—even if this means they say no to him. I still believe that one day my friends will come back. But they will be back on God's timetable, not on mine. In the meantime, we have seen the church rebuilt from the ashes, much stronger in its unity and purpose, with great, new young people, eager to save the nation.

Similarly, the story of John Emmanuel coming back to Jesus was very encouraging and exciting (chapter 15). Yet another dear friend who became a disciple in 1988 left the Lord a few years later. I prayed for him for many years, but he never came back to God. Instead, he had a very sad and difficult life and died two years ago. What I asked for in prayer did not come about.

Healthy Perspective

So what does all of this mean? Are our answered prayers simply random victories, having nothing to do with God? Is there no God who listens to us at all? This is how we are tempted to feel when God says no. But we must remember that while Jesus did not heal every single person who was sick in the first century, every miracle he performed was still special. So we too must rejoice in the miracles that God does bring about, knowing there is no earthly explanation for them. And at the same time, we must accept that when God says no, it must be in our best interest—even if we cannot understand it now.

Paul said in Romans 8:28, "And we know that in all things God works for the good of those who love him, who have been called according to his purpose." When God says no, we must not fall into depression or self-condemnation, searching endlessly for the flaw in our hearts that stopped him from saying yes. Nor should we question his faithfulness. Instead, we must rejoice in our relationship with him, trusting that his justice and judgement are flawless, and "we will understand it better, by and by."

Class Series

'The Prayer of the Righteous'

This book can easily be taught as a class series, covering usually two chapters per week, for ten weeks. Each week has a simple, specific challenge, aside from covering the material in the book. (Students should read the chapters to be covered in the class and answer the questions at the end of each chapter in addition to following the other suggestions below.)

Week 1
Introduction and Chapter 1
'I'm Going to Run to You'

This week, start having consistent prayers every day. Have a turning point in your relationship with God. Begin forming a habit of prayer for the next seven days that you can sustain for the rest of your life.

Week 2
Chapters 2 and 3
'I'll Crawl on My Knees for You and Forgive You'

This week, write a short essay (one to four pages) about your upbringing and how it has affected your view of God. Spread the paper out before the Lord, and talk to him about it. Share this essay with one of your close, spiritual friends.

Week 3

Chapters 4 and 5
'I'll Hold You Forever and Wipe Away Your Tears'

This week, talk to God about the hardest times in your life. Thank him for protecting you and carrying you through these times. Pray through the "Footprints" poem.

Week 4

Chapters 6 and 7
'You Are My Jewel; I'll Sing You a Love Song'

This week, find a piece of jewelry. Hold it in your hand and examine it. Pray to God about the times you have felt worthless. Thank him for loving you so much. Spend at least half an hour singing to him.

Week 5

Chapters 8 and 9
'The Holiness and Power of God'

This week, meet with another brother or sister and be open about your life. Have him or her be open, also. Pray together about your sin and about the holiness of God. Also, go to an inspiring spot (alone or with a friend) and praise God for his power.

Week 6

Chapter 10 and Appendix
'Heaven Is a Wonderful Place'; 'When God Says No'

[*Note to teacher:* teach the chapter, and then spend ten minutes or so asking participants what they think heaven will be like, and why (asking for Scriptural evidence for their ideas).] Also discuss how God sometimes says "No" or "Wait" when we pray. Spend at least half an hour in prayer, praising God for heaven.

Week 7

Chapter 11
'The ABCDs of Great Bible Study'

Take an hour or so to go through a passage in the Bible using the ABCD technique. Bring your work to class next week.

Week 8

Chapters 12 and 13
'Friendship with God and Mighty Faith'

This week, have a special time with God as a friend. Work on your relationship. Also, pray specifically every day, with faith, for God to do a particular miracle.

Week 9

Chapters 14 and 15
'Praising God and Getting His Attention'

Take at least half an hour to have a great time of praising God. Also, choose three things that you will aggressively pray for every day until God answers you. Write them down, and bring them in to class next week.

Week 10

Chapters 16 and 17
'Keeping It Fresh and Moving God's Heart'

Do something in your prayer time this week that you have never done before. Also, pray with passion about something. Pray God will soften your heart until your tears flow.

SCRIPTURE MEMORY
(for advanced students, or as the teacher decides)

Week 1

✱✱James 5:16 ~Confess~pray

Genesis 5:24 *Enochs* *walk*

Psalm 50:21b *we walk*

Luke 15:4 *find / sheep*

Luke 15:20 *Lost son*

Week 2

Psalm 18:35

Psalm 40:2

Psalm 66:18

Luke 15:8

Matthew 18:35

Week 3

Isaiah 40:11

Job 36:15

Matthew 11:28

1 Peter 5:7

Revelation 21:4

Week 4

Isaiah 43:4

Isaiah 49:16

Isaiah 62:3

Zephaniah 3:17

Matthew 10:31

Week 5

2 Chronicles 6:18

Isaiah 6:5

Isaiah 40:12

Ephesians 3:20-21

Hebrews 12:29

Week 6

Job 40:8

Isaiah 57:1

John 14:1-2

2 Corinthians 12:9

Revelation 21:2

Week 7

John 1:1

John 17:3

1 Corinthians 2:9-10

Philippians 3:10

Ephesians 6:18

Week 8

Exodus 33:11

Psalm 81:10

Isaiah 65:24

Jeremiah 30:21b

Mark 11:24

Week 9

Genesis 32:26

2 Chronicles 20:21

Psalm 100:4

Isaiah 62:6b-7

Colossians 4:12

Week 10

2 Kings 19:14

Jeremiah 17:8

Luke 19:41

John 11:35

Hebrews 5:7

Bibliography

Bonhoeffer, Dietrich. *The Psalms: The Prayer Book of the Bible*. Trans. James H. Burtness. Minneapolis: Augsburg, 1974.

Bridges, Jerry. *The Joy of Fearing God*. Colorado Springs: Waterbrook Press, 1997.

Cox, Douglas Ed and Edward A. Elliott, Sr., eds. *The Best of Andrew Murray on Prayer*. Uhrichsville, Ohio: Barbour Publishing, Inc., 1997.

Foster, Richard J. *Prayer: Finding the Heart's True Home*. London: Hodder & Stoughton, Ltd., 1992.

Law, William. *The Spirit of Prayer and the Spirit of Love*. Edited by Sidney Spencer. Canterbury: Clarke, 1969.

Levi, Primo. *Survival at Auschwitz*. Translated by Stuart Woolf. London: Simon & Schuster, 1993.

Lucado, Max. *Six Hours One Friday*. Portland, Oregon: Multnomah Press, 1989.

Petre, Kelly and Dede, eds. *Our God Is an Awesome God*. Boston: Discipleship Publications International, 1999.

Spurgeon, C. H. "Encouragements to Prayer," (sermon July 9, 1888) London: Passmore & Alabaster, 1894.

Who Are We?

Discipleship Publications International (DPI) began publishing in 1993. We are a nonprofit Christian publisher affiliated with the International Churches of Christ, committed to publishing and distributing materials that honor God, lift up Jesus Christ and show how his message practically applies to all areas of life. We have a deep conviction that no one changes life like Jesus and that the implementation of his teaching will revolutionize any life, any marriage, any family and any singles household.

Since our beginning we have published nearly 100 titles; plus we have produced a number of important, spiritual audio products. More than one million volumes have been printed, and our works have been translated into more than a dozen languages—international is not just a part of our name! Our books are shipped regularly to every inhabited continent.

To see a more detailed description of our works, find us on the World Wide Web at www.dpibooks.org. You can order books by calling 1-888-DPI-BOOK twenty-four hours a day. From outside the US, call 781-937-3883, ext. 231 during Boston-area business hours.

We appreciate the hundreds of comments we have received from readers. We would love to hear from you. Here are other ways to get in touch:

Mail: DPI, One Merrill St., Woburn, MA 01801
E-mail: dpibooks@icoc.org

Find Us on the
World Wide Web

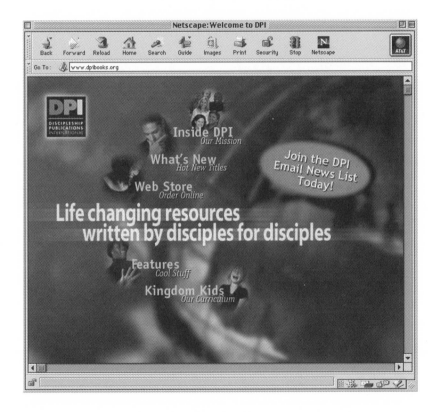

www.dpibooks.org
1-888-DPI-BOOK
outside US: 781-937-3883 x231